Music for children

Orff-Schulwerk
American Edition
Volume 1
Pre-School
based on
Carl Orff-Gunild Keetman
Musik für Kinder

SMC 12

Contributions by
Tossi Aaron · Millie Burnett · Isabel Carley · Virginia Ebinger · Nancy Ferguson · Ruth Pollock Hamm · Maureen Kennedy · Marcia Lunz · Dorothy Lyons · Erik Nielsen · Sue Ellen Page · Martha Pline · Arvida Steen · Judith Thomas · Lillian Yaross

Articles by
Maureen Kennedy · Marcia Lunz · Virginia McGivern · Martha Pline · Arvida Steen · Lillian Yaross

Co-ordination
Hermann Regner (Orff-Institute Salzburg)

MUSIC FOR CHILDREN VOLUME 1
ORFF-SCHULWERK American Edition

ISBN 0-930448-12-X

Printed in U.S.A.

Contents

Foreword

This is the last of the three volumes of the American Edition of Orff-Schulwerk to appear. The order of publication of the volumes was chosen according to the demand for materials at the particular age-levels for which the books were intended, hence the order 2-3-1. Most children who work with the ideas of Orff-Schulwerk are in the primary grades. The sequence of publication was also dictated by the material presented. The contributors were asked to submit only texts, songs, instrumental pieces, games and sample lessons that had originated from their practical work and which had been tried out many times.

A special problem for this edition arose from the fact that we wanted to realize the principle of Schulwerk by starting with traditional rhymes and songs. The layman often mistakenly thinks that these texts and melodies are in the public domain: Legally speaking, they are not! – in the case of virtually every little song taken from a published collection of some kind, we have had to enter into copyright negotiations, in some instances lasting a few years. For this reason, and because of the amount of material to be considered, publication has been delayed.

All three volumes and a number of supplements are now available. Our task has been to enrich the singing, playing and dancing of our children with a variety of material and plenty of methodological hints for the teacher. We have decided not to arrange the material as in other editions of Orff-Schulwerk (I Pentatonic, II Major: Drone Bass Triads, etc). Many other aspects were considered, one being the age of the children. We purposely chose the titles "Pre-school", "Primary" and "Upper-elementary" for the three volumes. This should not be understood as a limitation for teaching purposes, but should serve as a guideline. We have compiled the material considering the following questions:

1. What is of interest to the child? How is the child motivated? What can we offer to the child that will relate to his inner and outer world? What is necessary to guide the child's inclinations, preferences and interests in good time toward persons, situations, objects, feelings and thoughts about which he is not yet aware?

2. What kind of texts, songs, dances, games can challenge the child to active participation with which he can identify?

3. What kind of facilities are we assuming to be available (instruments, room space, schedules) and what do we expect *should* be made available?

All of these questions have been considered in arranging the choice and sequence of material in the three volumes. We all know, however, that education cannot be dictated, made uniform or decided upon as final. It is therefore necessary for those teachers planning to make use in the classroom of some of the material presented here to select in accord with their own teaching situation. What is of interest to my children? What are their needs? What can I convey to them convincingly?

These volumes, unlike other books for schools, should not be followed page by page from beginning to end.

A teacher makes a choice and is then responsible for the depth and breadth of the learning experience he has chosen for the children. Either an exhaustive study of a particular subject area in which much work is devoted to such details as technique, proper pronunciation, etc, or simply a very broad experience in singing or playing or dancing that lends itself to the spontaneity of the moment without fussing too much about such things as proper handing or left foot instead of right. The teaching processes should be varied frequently.

Each volume is divided into three parts. A progression from part to part and from volume to volume is clearly noticeable. These divisions were made taking into account the ability to reproduce, the development of co-ordination, the memory, the ability to express oneself spontaneously in music and movement, and the growing interest in reading and notating music and dance.

These volumes *do* follow the tradition of Orff-Schulwerk editions in other countries in that they offer models for the active participation of the whole class. We should like to make it clear, however, that this should not solely promote "learning by doing". John Dewey did not mean it like that when he defined this phrase; nor did Carl Orff and Gunild Keetman when they published the first volume of the German edition more than thirty years ago. The "doing" which is emphasized in this age-group can be reason, the motivation to think and to consider how things are made and how they function (Dewey).[1] Doing can also be the practical application and proof that a thing has been learned (still provoking new developments), that it has been internalized, practiced, and that this particular experience can be recalled and repeated.

One more word about learning. During the past century, American psychologists concerned with learning have repeatedly defined their understandings. Studying these definitions carefully, one observes that very few of them are concerned with the media of music and dance. Learning which results in a change of behavior through experience does not exist in general but only when there are specific tasks involved. Learning music is a different task from learning meaningless syllables or spatial relationships. Different procedures, different human dimensions, paths and goals have to be considered in the realm of fundamental education in music and dance. Obviously good music and movement training fosters and trains the child's social behavior, independence, readiness to communicate and to co-operate, emotional development and the ability to give expression to feelings and experiences. This training also furthers general awareness, concentration and memory, experiencing the movement possibilities of the body and spatial awareness. Even such phenomena as fantasy and creativity – which are difficult to measure – have been proven to be favorably influenced by Orff-Schulwerk.[2] All these

[1] *John Dewey,* Problems of Men, *New York 1946*
[2] *Revers, W. and Rauhe, H.,* Musik-Intelligenz-Phantasie, *Salzburg 1978*

behavior patterns, which are important for the entire human development and decisive for our survival, are practiced also in other areas of formal and informal learning. In addition to these important factors our main concern is music and dance. These media are not simply vehicles for a change of human behavior — which may very well be abandoned at the next turning-point when they are no longer needed — but they are, in all world cultures, as important for survival as water and air. Man becomes an entity again when he makes music and when he dances: he uses his hands and feet, his body, his senses, his intellect and emotion. He experiences the challenge of being permitted a certain freedom while at the same time experiencing the natural order of things.

Music and dance are not a world unto themselves, nor an oasis in the midst of our troubled world. They are documentations of one of man's characteristic facets of being, a part of an entity which needs constant renewal.

Hermann Regner

The story of the Three Billy Goats Gruff is well known to many children. The following photographs show children re-enacting the tale with song and accompaniment.

I'm feeling very hungry, I think I'll take a walk.

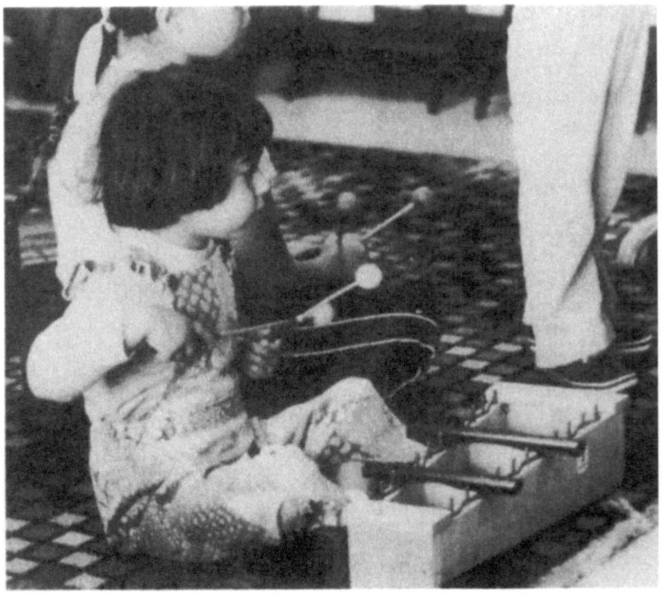

Trit trot, trit trot.

Beware, beware!

I'm going to eat you up!

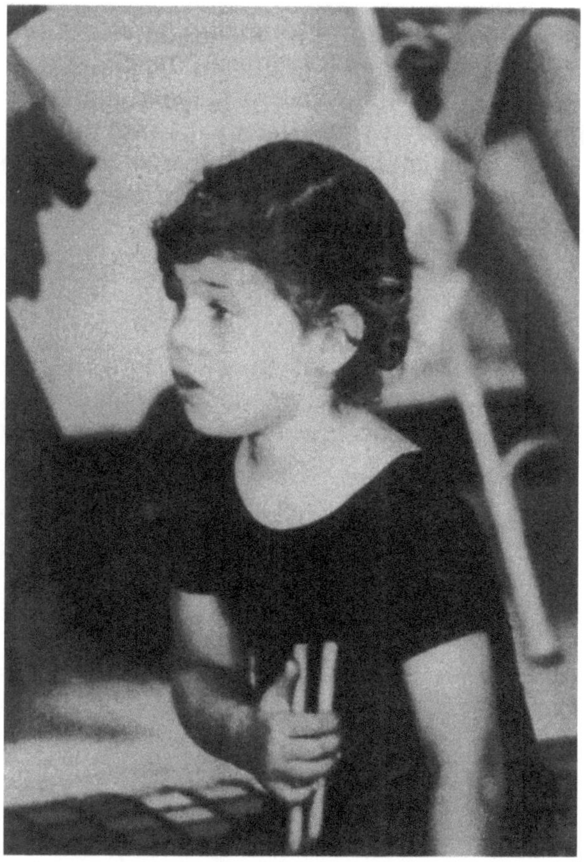

**Please don't eat me, Mr Troll.
Wait for my big brother.**

AN EXPLANATION OF SOME TERMINOLOGY IN THIS EDITION INCLUDING ABBREVIATIONS

Bar Instruments

Soprano Glockenspiel	SG
Alto Glockenspiel	AG
Soprano Xylophone	SX
Alto Xylophone	AX
Bass Xylophone	BX
Soprano Metallophone	SM
Alto Metallophone	AM
Bass Metallophone	BM

Recorders

Sopranino Recorder	Si. R
Soprano Recorder	Sopr. R
Alto Recorder	Alto R
Tenor Recorder	Ten. R
Bass Recorder	Bass R

Voice	V
Violoncello	Vc

Timpani, drums and other percussion instruments

Bass drum	BD
Bongo drums	Bong
Claves	Cl
Conga drums	Cong
Cymbals	C
Finger cymbals	FC
Guiro or Reco-reco	G
Hand drum	HD
Hanging cymbal	HC
Maracas or rattles	Mar
Sleigh bells or bells	SB
Tambourine	Tamb
Timpani	T
Triangle	Tr
Wood block	WB

Mallets

With wooden or hard rubber heads ●
Of felt or other soft material ○

Synopsis of keys and compasses

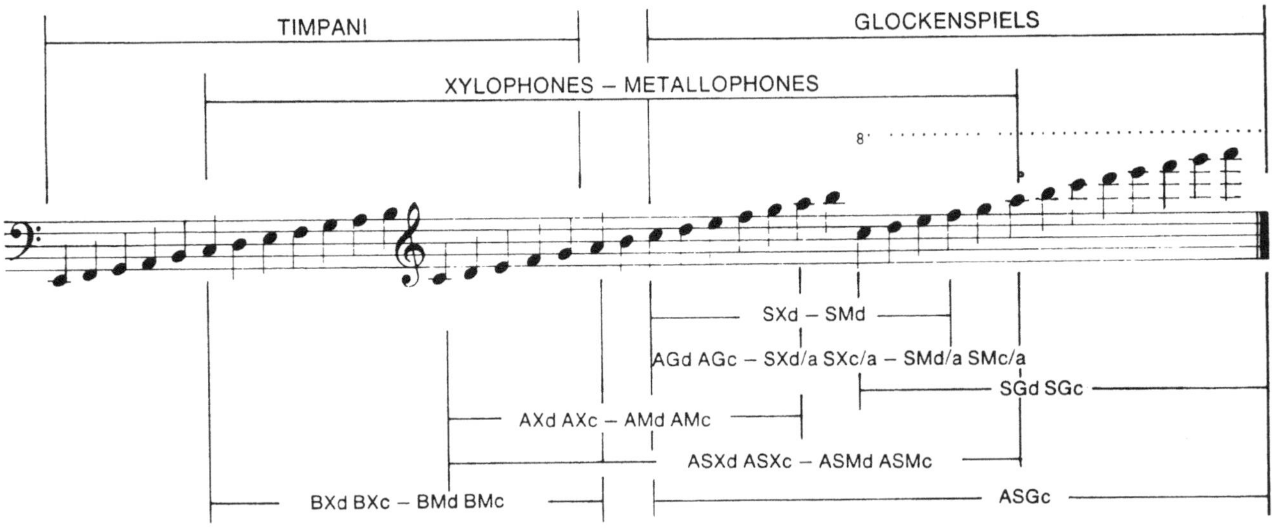

Sound Gestures
The separate or combined actions of finger snapping, hand clapping, thigh slapping, foot stamping.

Patsch
A German word for which there is no succinct English equivalent, describing the sound gesture of thigh slapping. In this edition the word has been anglicized to include the forms: patsching, patsched, etc.

Patsching
Slapping the thighs with one or both hands in a relaxed and bouncing way. It is used in rhythmic exercises and for the preparation of instrumental playing.

Non-pitched instruments
Small percussion instruments that have no definite pitch (claves, wood block, tambourine, hand drum, rattle, sleigh bells, cymbals, etc).

Ostinato
The persistent, obstinate (Lat. *obstinatus)* repetition of a clearly defined rhythmic, melodic or harmonic structure. In Fundamental Music and Movement Education the ostinato plays an important part as accompaniment for pentatonic and modal melodies which do not require a harmonic accompaniment. This form of accompaniment has certain advantages when it comes to teaching, one of them being that a number of players can learn their parts quickly without having to use printed notation. Experience has proven that ostinato playing, especially with young children, needs a lot of attention and discipline.

Bordun
Bordun (Lat. *bordunus,* Ital. *bordone,* Eng. drone bass) is an ostinato form of accompaniment in which only the first and fifth tones in any given key are sounded.

Explanatory Notes

☐ This edition is intended as a teachers' guide. Not only does it contain a rich collection of material but also many suggestions for use in the course of teaching. When the individual teacher is in agreement with these suggestions, then they may be used as they stand. If the teacher feels that because of personality or for reasons of particular classroom situations it would be better to make a change, then it is right to do so.

☐ The pedagogical suggestions are not recipes to be followed ingredient for ingredient, but on the one hand are intended to ease the task of the teacher and on the other are merely comments from the contributors about their own experiences. All pieces have been proven in classes with children. It may happen that many of the examples can be worked out with children rather quickly in a short period of time; others may need longer periods of preparation for development.

☐ Some of the songs in this edition, especially those of folk origin, are known in other melodic forms. Choose the melody you are familiar with, or the one the children know in their particular area.

☐ It is possible to combine different pieces for purposes of creating a larger music and/or movement form. A song, for example, followed by an instrumental piece in similar or contrasting character can extend the form.

☐ It was especially difficult to make a decision concerning the notation for bass instruments. Parts for bass xylophone and bass metallophone have been written in the treble clef with an octave sign below to facilitate a change to another instrument if necessary. In addition, the use of the treble clef makes it easier to comprehend the full score at a glance. The notation for timpani remains in the bass clef. It is also possible to use plucked or bowed stringed instruments as bass parts, (guitar, lute, gamba, cello).

☐ There are some instruments whose tonal quality is such that it is extremely difficult to blend with the Orff instrumentarium, e.g. melodicas or electronic instruments; therefore it is recommended that they are not used in this way.

☐ We do not repeat here many of the familiar, traditional singing games for children (London Bridge; Mulberry Bush; Oats, Peas, Beans and Barley, etc). However it should be understood that these games have an important place in music and movement education and should be played often.

Identification Symbols

Sample Lesson

Game

Listening Activity

Notation Skills

Photographs

The photographs in this book show Orff-Schulwerk in American classrooms.

We thank the following individuals and institutions for their contributions:

	page
Marilyn Blanc, San Francisco Conservatory	II + III
Tossi Aaron	9
Don Slagel, Colby College, Waterville, Maine	10
Tossi Aaron	13
Tossi Aaron	19
Carol Erion, The Montessori School, Annandale, Virginia	48
Donald Slagel, Colby College, Waterville, Maine	52
Marilyn Blanc, San Francisco Conservatory	54 (left)
Tossi Aaron	54 (right)
Marcia Lunz	64-68

PART 1

Games represent most of the contributions in this section (see Introduction). They are intended to help the child develop a feeling for becoming part of a group and to prepare him for a social kind of playing and learning. These games combine activities in speech, music and movement.

Singing makes use of the following tonal combinations (listed in pitch from highest to lowest):

so-mi	la-so-mi-re-do
la-so	so-fa-mi-re-do
la-so-mi	re-do-la-so
mi-re-do	mi-re-do-so
do'-la-so	mi-re-do-la-so
la-so-mi-re	so-fa-mi-re-do-ti-so
so-mi-re-do	so-mi-re-do-la-so
re'-do'-la-so	do'-la-so-mi-re-do

Songs are in the keys of C, G and F major. Because most of the songs are pentatonic (without fa and ti) the key signatures are in many instances really unnecessary. They are given here as an aid to the teacher in determining the tonality. There are also melodic lines which introduce the mood and structure of minor tonalities. To achieve the best results when singing with young children, the following suggestions may be helpful:

- do not sing too loudly
- sing in a range that is not too low in pitch
- make frequent changes between singing alone and with others, accompanied and unaccompanied

Since the teacher's voice will be imitated by the child, it is important for that person to consider the aspects of proper breathing, diction, support and expression.

Listening Experiences offer first acquaintances with pitch discrimination, contrasting timbres and lengths of phrases.

Reading and Writing Music begins with movement games and graphic representation of sounds.

Instrumental Playing is not required at this time. Occasionally the teacher may accompany on various instruments to motivate the children for their own playing at a later stage.

1. Name Play

When a child meets other children, his name establishes his identity in the group. Often the child "knows" another child when he knows his name. Name play in many variations secures the child's place and recognition in the group. The teacher should be aware of this psychological phenomenon in evaluating and ascertaining the educational use of names of the children. Names, like other words, allow the first experience with the rhythmic aspect of language.

1. Group seated in a circle. First speak each name. Second time in turn with a steady beat. Let the language flow in a natural tempo. (Be careful not to distort the name to fit the beat.) Then names are repeated by the group. Each child says his name in solo. In another variation, names may be sung in so-mi pattern.

2. **Ring around the Rosie**
   Play with small groups. Call each child in turn to fall down. "John, John, John fall down."

3. Chant together in a circle
   Group: "Name, name , what's your name?
   Ask me again and I'll tell you the same."
   Solo: "Nancy"
   Group: "Nancy"

4. Seated in a circle, patsch the beat:
   Group: "Rickety, rackety, rockety, ree
   Will you say your name to me?"
   Solo: "George"
   Group: "George"

2. Cuckoo

Formation
Seated circle with "It" and "Cuckoo" in center.

Game
The song is sung three times while the blindfolded child, "It", turns in a circle in place. Some children may be frightened of being blindfolded. The teacher should be sensitive to each child's reaction and judge when one is ready to take a turn and how long the "cuckoo search" should last.

Bordun continues softly (length of song three times) while "It" tries to find "Cuckoo" from the ringing sound of the finger cymbal, triangle, or hanging cymbal, which "Cuckoo" holds and strikes as he moves to different locations in the room. After "Cuckoo" is found, "Cuckoo" and blindfolded child choose two other children to take their places and the game continues.

An introduction and/or interlude may be added by class members echoing teacher's "Cuckoo" when she touches them on the head, e.g. teacher moves around outside of the circle so that the children's backs are to the teacher. She may touch one or several children's heads while she sings her "Cuckoo". It is suggested that the "Cuckoos" be varied in dynamics and rhythm in order to present a musical setting for the game.

3. Riddle Me

(hair)

Other riddles for singing with two tones.

Thirty white horses
upon a white hill:
now they dance,
now they prance,
now they stand still.

(teeth)

A house full,
a hole full,
you cannot gather
a bowl full.

(mist)

From The Puffin Book of Nursery Rhymes *gathered by Iona and Peter Opie, Penguin, 1963, p. 72.*

4. Singing Stories

- ☐ to stimulate the melodic imagination
- ☐ to encourage good vocal production
- ☐ to heighten awareness of pitch
- ☐ to help children perceive speech as a precursor of song

1 – Begin by greeting the class, calling the roll, or making preliminary comments by singing instead of speaking, varying the melodic line to suit the topic in a clear but simple way.

2 – Ask questions and encourage the children to answer in song, without comment on the pitch or melodic inventiveness: just let it happen in a comfortable way.

3 – Choose a familiar story to dramatize and sing, preferably one with very well-established dialog (like The Three Bears) to help the shy ones. Act out the story in groups, matching the movement style to the character so that all have parts.

4 – Another time, add simple props or suggestions of costumes such as scarves or hats.

5 – Eventually, the children can make small groups, and go off on their own to work out various stories in song to present to each other at the end.

6 – This may also be done with simple pantomimes of familiar actions, like going to the store, taking a walk, etc, simultaneously singing the description of everything seen or done as it happens.

5. Wee Willie Winkie

Here is an example of a rich score of accompaniment for a nursery rhyme. Such an instrumentation can only be realized after the children have had some experience with Orff Instruments. Many other versions are possible.

Margaret Murray: "Wee Willie Winkie" *and Seven Other Songs using three and four notes with easy accompaniments Schott Ed. 10916, London*

6. Bounce the Ball to Jericho

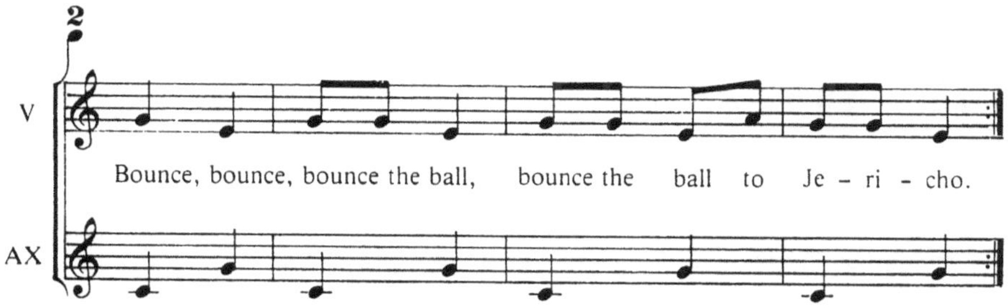

Bounce the Ball to Jericho
The skills involved in this game would need to be developed over a period of several lessons. Some preceding activities might include:

- ☐ a movement session bouncing and moving freely around the room with the ball.*
- ☐ have children sit in a circle and pass the ball on the teacher's drum beat from child to child. When the "passing" begins to fall into a steady rythm the teacher may add a change of direction in passing when she taps the rim of the drum.
- ☐ add words "pass, pass, pass the ball, pass the ball to Jericho"
- ☐ teacher and/or child moves to the center of the circle and rolls the ball, on the pulse, to a child in the outer circle who without breaking the rythm, rolls the ball back to the center person. Play proceeds around the circle with the word "pass" changing to "roll, roll, roll the ball . . ."
- ☐ the teacher now bounces the ball from the inside to the outside circle, as stated above. When children really become accomplished at this, the teacher may bounce the ball to a child anywhere in the outer circle– behind her, to the side, etc. This calls for quick reaction, very close attention and very good co-ordination.

**The ball should be similar in size to the balls used in P.E. classes (8½" or 10").*

7. The Penny Game

(V)  or (V) 

Leader: "Who has the penny?"
"Who has the keys?"
"Who has the paper-clip?"
"Who has the triangle?"
"Who has the crayon?"
"Who has the eraser?"

1st child: "I have the penny."
2nd child: "I have the keys."
3rd child: "I have the paper-clip."
4th child: "I have the triangle."
5th child: "I have the crayon."
6th child: "I have the eraser."

Small group of 6 to 8 children sit around an array of commonly found objects, such as those above. LEADER closes eyes tightly as each child quickly takes one object and hides it behind her back. LEADER then sings the question for each object. The child who has it holds it up, sings the reply and places it in the center again. EVERY-ONE SHOULD HAVE A TURN TO BE A LEADER!

Large group
Have an aide or helper gently tap the first five or six children to get a turn at picking up an object from the center pile. Last one to answer gets to be leader. Continue the game until everyone has a turn to pick up an item and sing an answer.

See Volume 2, No. 86, p. 63, for another variation of this game.

8. Elevator

Playing "elevator" can help children act out high and low sounds. The teacher or a child calls out "Basement!" or one of the upper floors, and the children crouch, rise or stop accordingly.

City children may choose to be in a very tall building or a department store with different items for sale on each floor.

This may be shown graphically with chalk lines on the board, colored lines on paper, or blocks stacked on each other. Some may move while others draw, changing places after a few turns.

Those moving as well as those drawing can use their voices to accompany their movements and their drawing. There can be an elevator operator or it can be a self-operating one, with the number of the floor indicated with a wood block or triangle.

9. Hot Cross Buns

Ask the children to clap (or play an instrument) each time they sing 'Hot cross buns".

10. Suo-Gân (See-oh-gahn)

2. Suogân, Eastern Star,
   Suogân, from afar;
   Suogân, shepherds sing,
   Suogân, newborn King.
3. Suogân, from above,
   Suogân, song of love;
   Suogân, blessed morn,
   Suogân, Christ is born.

The children may make up more verses to the song!

11. Vihmakene, Vellekene (Rain, my little brother)

Estonia

Children hum this melody, or sing it on the syllable lah or loo. They can patsch the beat in imitation of different sized raindrops: 𝅗𝅥 for large drops, ♩ for medium sized ones, and ♫ for light, fast rain. As an introduction and an interlude, also as an accompaniment, children improvise "rain music". Select different instruments and experiment with the sounds.

The text of the complete song in English (translated by Reet Hendrikson):

Rain, my little brother rain.
Don't fall on the shepherd boy.

I have no home where I can dry.
I have no house where I can find shelter.

My home is under the oak tree leaf.
The pine tree will give me shelter.

12. "Leo and Lamb Chop"

Exercises in Pitch Discrimination

Leo and Lamb Chop are velour hand-puppets who live in a box on the shelf (where the lion lies down with the lamb!). They could, of course, have any names the children wish to give them. They are a means of reinforcing pitch concepts on a continuing basis.

When they are first introduced, they speak in characteristic high and low voices. The teacher reminds the children that like big grown men, Leo has a low voice, because he is a large animal, and that Lamb Chop, being much smaller, as children are, has a high one. The children make deep roars and high bleats. Such activity can function as a starting point for movement improvisation, with stress on the size of the animals and their qualities of movement.

On some days, the puppets, on the hands of the teacher or a child, can lead the speaking of heritage rhymes; the task being to change one's voice as the animals change. Dynamics should not be neglected. Both animals can speak either loudly or softly!

Singing can be pitched low by Leo, or high by Lamb Chop – a helpful device to encourage those children whose natural voices lie in an extreme range. Singing in this way works well only with two or three pitch songs; otherwise, out-of-tune singing is produced. Of course, in singing, the children are not expected to switch back and forth between high and low.

Later – with mallets held in their mouths – the two animals progress to playing instruments. Lamb Chop plays finger cymbals, glockenspiel and finger drum, while Leo uses large suspended cymbal, bass metallophone and bass drum or timpani. The animals conduct children who are playing "their" instruments (varying dynamics, of course). Or the children may be shown two instruments and asked to choose the proper animal to play.

As the children's discrimination becomes more acute, Leo and Lamb Chop sit on opposite ends of one instrument, and finally play high and low octaves of the same instrument. They sit at opposite ends of the piano, where they point out that the length of the string accounts for its pitch.

The children like playing with the animals in their free time, using the characteristic voices. With any given group of children the puppets take on distinct personalities, and children enjoy them long after their educational function is gone.

13. Little Jack Jingle

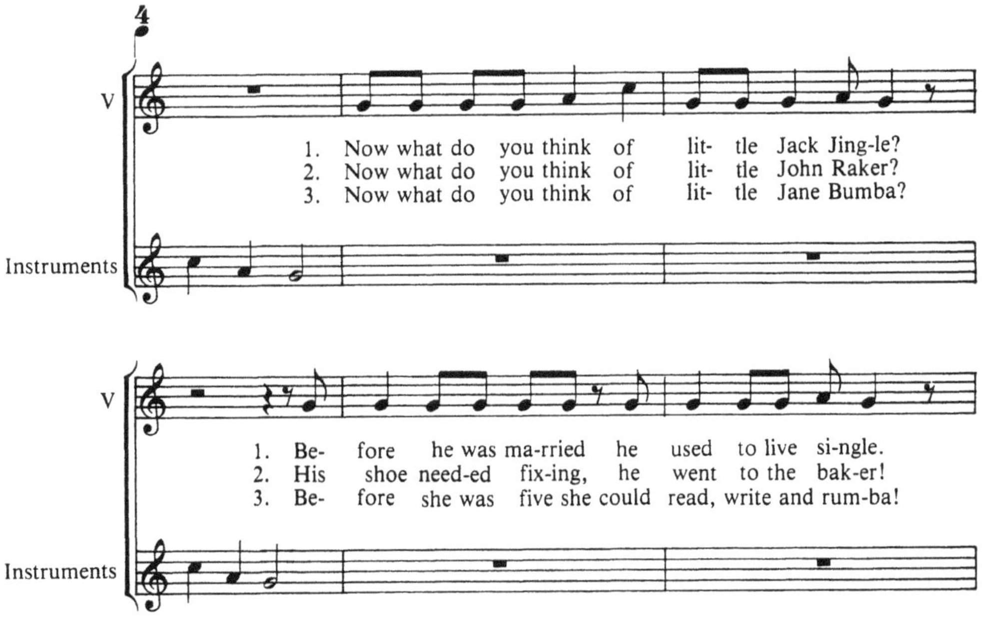

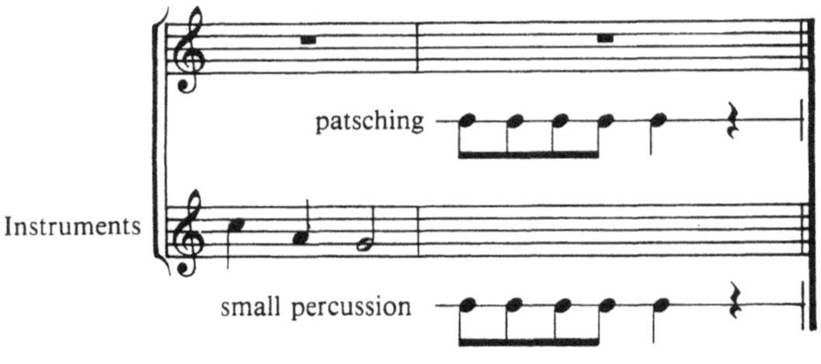

First verse from The Puffin Book of Nursery Rhymes, *Iona and Peter Opie, Penguin, 1963.*
Second and third verses, Virginia McGivern.

14. Circle Travel Game

- ☐ to provide for imitative movement as leader and follower
- ☐ review locomoter movements: walk, run, skip, hop, jump, crawl, gallop, etc.

Further movement exploration can deal with varying basic locomoter movements by adding the dimension of high or low, narrow or wide, smooth or jerky.

Game

Players sit in a circle. One child walks around the outside of the circle while the song is sung. On the last word of the song, the child stops behind someone in the circle. This player then shows the first a new way to move (gallop, crawl, hop, sidestep, etc). The first child follows and imitates the movement and takes the place just vacated. The song begins again and the second child walks around the circle as the game continues.

Should the leader stop behind someone who has already been a leader, the leader can walk forward to the next child who has not been up.

15. Spool and Key

Formation
Seated circle, children with eyes closed and hands behind them—palms up.

Game
The song is sung twice while two people (one with the spool and one with the key) skip around behind children in seated circle and place the spool and the key in the hands of two other children. The teacher or class member then sings: "Who has the spool?" and child sings: "I have the spool." The teacher then sings the same question to the child with the key and the key child responds. The class tries to guess who has the spool and the key from the individual's sung answers. Game may be repeated as often as desired.

The child's eyes should remain closed during the question and answers and opened only for the guessing part of the game.

16. Playtime Chants

Climbed a hickory,
shinned a pine,
tore my britches
right behind.

I had a mule and his name was Jack,
rode his tail to save his back.

I had a little dog and his name was Rover.
When he died, he died all over.

Monkey sittin' on the end of a rail,
pickin' his teeth with the end of his tail.

Amen, Brother Ben
shot a goose and killed a hen.

17. Several Animals

Several animals are discussed, with particular attention to their size, length of leg and tempo of movement (a visit to the zoo helps). After the children have had an opportunity to explore these many ways of moving on their own, small percussion instruments are chosen to initiate the movement. Initially, these may be played by the teacher, and later by the children. The whole class can respond to the instruments, or small groups can choose one of the animals and move about the room accompanied by the instrument player. Another time, a specific rhythm pattern may emerge for each of the animals.

Example: Wood block  Frog

Guiro  Caterpillar

Tom-tom  Camel

18. Order in the Court

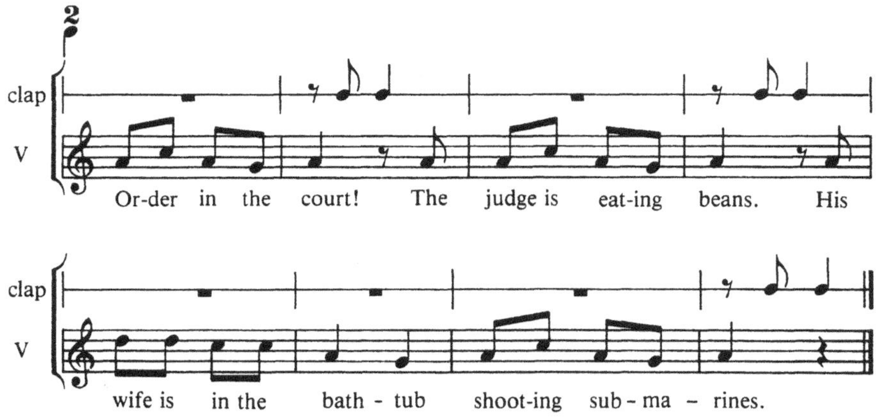

Words: Traditional American.
Source: Junior Voices, *edited by Geoffrey Summerfield, the first book, Penguin.*

19. Up and Down

Teacher plays recorder or xylophone glissandi or single notes in ascending or descending scale patterns. The playing is quiet, deliberate and as legato as possible. Children move up or down according to the sound they hear. At first it is best not to change the direction in the middle. (1) Later, when the children become more discriminating listeners, surprise changes are fun. (2) The tempo may be varied and *should* be varied, as much as possible during this activity.

The musical examples below are suggestions. There are other instruments well suited to this activity, including the voice!

(1) Xylophone glissandi—felt or wooden sticks

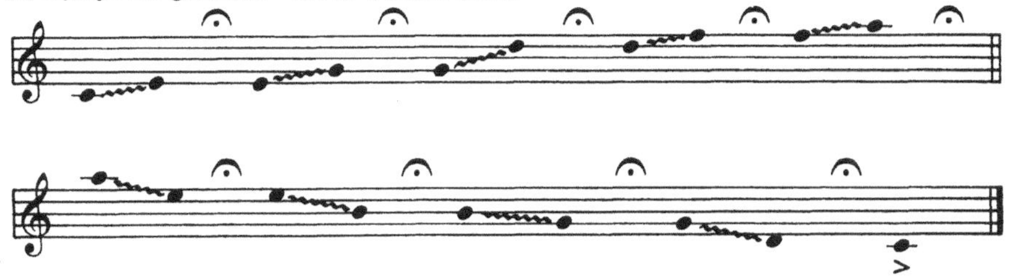

(1) Soprano recorder (Transpose to F major for Alto recorder)

(2) Xylophone glissandi

(2) Recorder—tempo ad libitum

20. Johnny works with One Hammer

This is a "follow the leader" game which helps children play a steady pulse while singing. It is best done while sitting.

1. Teacher begins song with right fist playing the beat on right knee.
   Second time, both fists playing on both knees . . .
   Third time, add one foot tapping . . .
   Fourth time, add two feet tapping . . .
   Fifth time, add head nodding.
2. Transfer progressive body motions to different unpitched percussion instruments.
3. A transfer can be made to barred instruments using a combination of tonic and dominant chords. This is good practice for alternating mallets as a further development for older children:

21 Traveling

Old game adapted, tune changed
(original was "Pop Goes the Weasel")

A circle of children decides on a place and a means of transportation, e.g. airplane, bicycle, rowboat or train. Some discussion of the relative tempi of the vehicles might follow.

With hands joined, the circle moves to the right, singing the place name and vehicle. The tune is repeated with "la-la" or an appropriate sound as the circle reverses direction, and imitates the vehicle in pantomime. Some popular ones are arms outstretched for a plane, turning around for a helicopter, fast shuffle for a train. Besides adjusting the speed and intensity of gesture, the children's task is to perceive the end of the pantomime and join hands for the next verse. In a small group, each child can have a turn to name the place and the means of transportation.

Another time, a large group could divide into several smaller circles.

(This makes a nice canon if each succeeding group enters after one measure!)

22. Name Play—2

1. Jim bum bim,
   Tilly ko tim,
   Tee-legged, ty-legged,
   Bow-legged Jim.

   Annie bum bannie,
   Tilly ko tannie,
   Tee-legged, ty-legged,
   Bow-legged Annie.

   Mary bum bary,
   Tilly ko tary,
   Tee-legged, ty-legged,
   Bow-legged Mary.

2. What's your name?
   Puddin' Tame.
   Ask me again and I'll tell you the same.

Use of this verse in name play may have the consequence that children tease each other with it. Be sure to include the teacher's name in the game.

23. Footprints

Using a man's shoe as a pattern, trace and cut out about two dozen "footprints" from colored paper. Have the children do the same with their own feet until there are at least forty-eight.

After some discussion and experiments with the differences in length of stride and tempo, the "feet" are taped securely to a smooth floor. They might be arranged in two parallel paths, two long lines, or crossing each other. The children take turns trying to step the paths. Later, two different percussion instruments are chosen to accompany those stepping.

Note: For safety on a carpeted floor, the "feet" can be cut from felt, muslin, or non-woven interfacing like "Pellon".

Variation: On a long piece of stage scenery paper, the children print their feet after having them rolled with poster paint by the teacher. (Outdoors!) Do this along one edge of the paper, and have an adult do the same along the other edge (in our school it was the principal who came out to see what we were doing!). These days children's sneakers have especially interesting patterns on them (which can lead to other projects with alike/different, matching pairs, design placement, etc. Once we "played" the colors of the prints, choosing an instrument for each, and orchestrating them!).

24. Stars Shining

1. Teacher sings and children listen, holding up number of fingers for each number sung.
2. The song is learned by children through imitation of melodic phrases.
3. Some children add tone clusters on glockenspiels for each number sung. Teacher adds bass xylophone.
4. Extension of counting game. Children take places on a number line, one-ten . . . As a given number is sung, child jumps forward. The song is then repeated in reverse order, as children jump back into place.

For another variation, see American Edition Vol. 2, No. 257, p.186.

25. High—Low

Two players are seated in the center of a circle, each one with an instrument, either high- or low-pitched, e.g. soprano glockenspiel and alto metallophone. Those in the circle respond to whichever instrument is played by curling into a ball, crouching, etc, or rising on tiptoe and stretching. The two center players agree in pantomime which of them will play, and the circle keeps eyes closed to heighten perception as it responds.

Later, or after some experience with this, one instrument can be played in stepwise patterns up or down to cue the movement. The instrument player can vary the tempo at will.

26. In the Evening when the Sun goes Down

27. The Ball Game

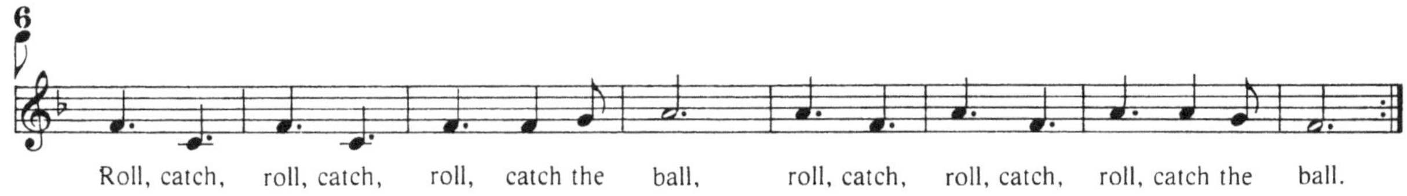

The children sit on the floor in a circle, with their legs tucked out of the way or spread wide. The teacher sings the song until the children are ready to join in. The tempo of the song is determined by the size of the circle since the point of the game is to match the movement of the ball to the words of the song.

When the song is familiar, let the children play with partners, one pair at a time, while the rest of the class marks the beat with simple improvised body rhythm patterns of their own invention.

Add a drum or timpani on the beat, if you wish, or an open fifth on BX on F and C if anyone can hold the pulse steady.

As the term progresses, change the game to "Bounce, catch", with the teacher in the middle of the circle, bouncing the ball to each child in turn.
Later, let a child be leader.
Later still, bounce the ball to any child who's watching, without any predetermined sequence. Again, let children take turns as leader.
Let one child challenge another to play "Bounce, catch" in the middle of the circle while the rest of the class follows a chosen leader in a simple body-rhythm pattern. The winner challenges another player, and so on, until the day's champion is left.

Later still, change the game to "Toss, catch", using a bean bag to start with, and shifting to a ball when the children are ready.

For variety, find other rhymes to use for the same game, or make up your own, like this:

Roll the ball,
roll the ball,
1, 2, 3,
roll the ball,
roll the ball,
roll it over to me.

Or use traditional ball-playing rhymes, like this:

Ungai, mungai,
chick-a chack-a chungai,
alligator, ungai,
over!

28. Postman

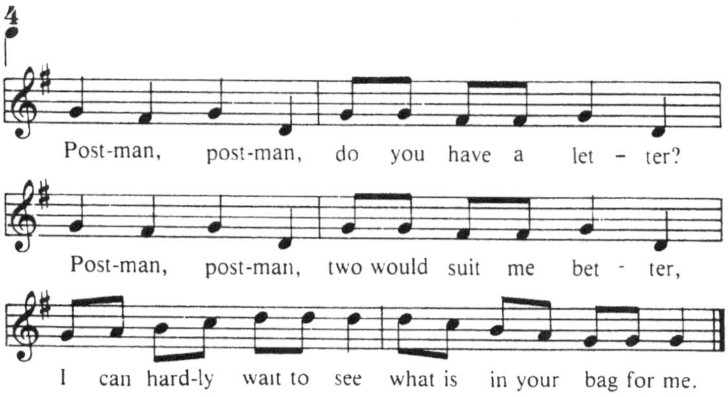

Little letters made of folded paper, one for each person in the group. Two are marked in some way perhaps with a star, and a heart, or other symbols. These are given out (from a basket or box) while the song is sung. Those holding marked letters become the next "postman" who gives out the letters, or the "mailbox" who collects them at the end or holds the basket for the mailman.

Variation: Little drawings of instruments can be on the letters as a means of choosing who will play what today. Many adaptations: characters of a story to act out, etc.

29. Scarves

- ☐ to learn to move in a smooth, fluid way
- ☐ to control the muscles in gliding and sliding
- ☐ to enlarge the movement vocabulary with a scarf

Inexpensive sheer nylon scarves from the dime store are needed, one for each child. These *must* be transparent like chiffon, and at least ½-meter square in light colors.

With the lights out, the children sit at random on the floor "in a little ball", that is, with knees up, head tucked in and down. Eyes are closed. In silence, an opened scarf is draped over each child's head. At a signal heads up, eyes open and the children stand slowly and begin to move around the room in their own ways, feeling the scarf move in the draft, etc. Whispered directions and slow movement will maintain the mood. Freely improvised sounds on cymbal, drum with brushes, triangle, sand blocks or maracas may be added or used as cues for forward, backward, stooping down and up, etc.

Eventually, the familiar activities with scarves may emerge: lifting high and spreading out low on floor, turning, running across room with it overhead, or inventing designs with a partner. However, the activity above has value and indeed magic for very small children, who are content to do it in a quiet, mysterious way at first.

30. Mary wore a Red Dress

Children sitting in a circle. The teacher sings someone's name, e.g. . . . "Christy wore a blue shirt, a blue shirt," etc.

Christy stands and skips around the circle while children clap and sing. "We will clap for Christy . . ."

Variation: Teacher sings:
"Who wore a blue shirt, a blue shirt," etc.

Children sing the answer:
"Christy wore a blue shirt," etc.

Accompaniment for song: Teacher playing bass xylophone or guitar with chordal accompaniment.

31. Marionettes

- ☐ to develop good co-ordination
- ☐ to increase awareness of the body parts and how they move
- ☐ to stimulate the imagination

Beginning with the children lying relaxed on the floor, face down, a story is related with piano improvisation as rhythmic impetus for the children's movement ideas.

Example

Once upon a time there lived a man and his wife in a little house at the edge of the forest. They were very lonely and always enjoyed talking with the children who came to the forest on picnics. One day, they decided to make some carved marionettes to surprise the children . . .

The story might continue to relate how the various parts are shaped, painted (especially the smile), strung together and are lying loosely in the box. One by one the strings are pulled and that part of the body begins to move . . . combinations like one hand and one leg, or head and one elbow, are good.

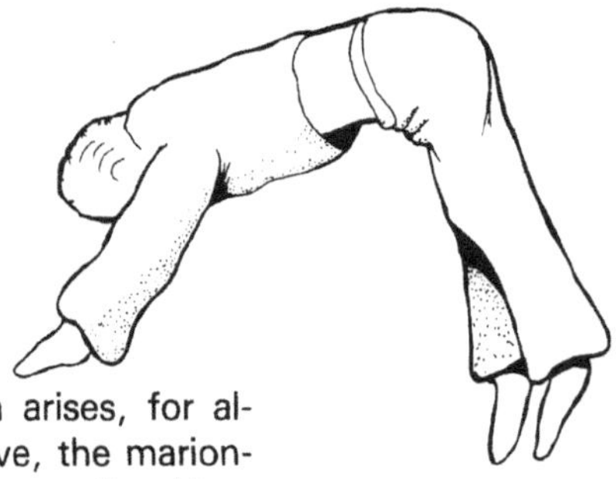

Eventually a problem arises, for although the parts move, the marionette will not stand . . . "problem thinking" music, and at last the solution . . . a string on the seat of the pants! This is tried, perhaps with a scale pattern on piano (later a xylophone), perhaps slipping out of the fingers once or twice, and finally adding all the other parts until all are standing, loosely in place. Special music of marionette dance, performance with curtain opening for the children to see, applause, etc.

"And they all lived happily ever after."

32. Kings and Queens

The children are scattered around the room in their usual places. One child is crowned king (or queen) and moves to the teacher's improvised phrase(s) until the music stops. At the end of the phrase (or period) the king must be in front of another child, ready to doff his beanbag crown by bowing his head so that the "crown" falls into the waiting child's hands. The chosen child is the next ruler, and the first king takes his place and sits down.

As the children become more expert listeners, the teacher can extend the phrases with unexpected little repetitions, or make the phrases of irregular length. In the beginning, the phrases will have to be very clearly balanced, and all the same length.

This game provides the teacher a good opportunity to introduce a variety of scales and a much wider range than the children are yet able to sing. Pentatonic tunes centered on LA or RE or SO, or modal tunes are particularly effective. The teacher's tunes must, of course, be dignified and legato, encouraging "royal" movement. (The beanbag crown helps too.)

With older children, let those who have already been kings or queens play a simple accompaniment with their choice of unpitched percussion, or, possibly, an open bordun on a bar instrument which has already been set up in an appropriate key.

33. Five Little Snowmen

Four little snowmen underneath the tree:
one more melted, then there were three.

Three little snowmen, with nothing to do:
one ran away, and then there were two.

Two little snowmen, having lots of fun:
one fell down, and then there was one.

One little snowman, standing very tall:
it rained and rained– then there were none at all.

This little song may be presented in several ways. The words offer a natural setting for dramatization. The dramatization may take place while the song is sung or used as a "B" section with children and the teacher providing an improvisational background. You may wish to stress the number concept by having each snowman, or additional children play five different unpitched instruments, representative of their number, during the song.

34. Reacting to Contrasting Timbres

Show children the suspended cymbal and the claves. Have children shut their eyes. Play a sound on an instrument and ask children to guess which instrument made the sound. After doing this several times, varying dynamics and playing techniques, discuss with the children the fact that different materials (wood and metal) make different kinds of sounds.

Have children again close their eyes and listen to the suspended cymbal several times. Then ask them to listen and put their hands up when "you don't hear the sound any more". After several tries, the children nearest to the cymbal should be the last to raise their hands. With the children's eyes still shut, repeat the procedure with the claves. Obviously, the hands will go up immediately.

Discuss with the children the fact that the claves sound is short and goes away quickly, while the cymbal sound lasts a long time. To underscore the latter, play a sound on the cymbal and hold it close to each child's ear in turn, so the children can hear the low vibrations which continue long after a person standing several feet away can no longer hear the sound.

With the children spaced around the room ask them to move their bodies as long as they hear each sound. Play a series of sounds first on cymbal, then claves. Allow plenty of time for cymbal sounds to die away. Children will probably make smooth slow movements for cymbal and short quick ones for claves. If they have difficulties with the former, suggest that they stretch their bodies in various directions on various levels.

Next the two types of sounds can be interspersed. Finally, the group can be divided into two groups, each reacting to one instrument, and freezing when the sound is over. The groups can be interspersed with each other, and a concrete image suggested. Perhaps those reacting to the cymbal could be trees waving in the breeze, while those reacting to the claves could be little woodland animals such as chipmunks.

35. A Poem to Play with

Plant four seeds when you make a row,
One to rot and one to grow
One for the pigeon and one for the crow.

Southern America

1. Decide what the poem means, then . . .
2. Enjoy and explore it rythmically by clapping it, patsching it, devising varied body percussions for the three lines, then further varying it through different dynamics and voice qualities.
3. Try clapping only the four key words: rot, grow, pigeon and crow, while the poem is spoken. Now internalize it, and saying the poem together silently, again clap only on the key words.
4. Find four instrumental sounds to represent rot, grow, pigeon and crow, and add them to the group reading of the poem (i.e., guiro scrape for "rot" etc).
5. With the children invent a melody for the poem, possibly limiting to C pentatonic. To this add a bordun bass accompaniment.
6. Put all the pieces together thus far: song with non-tonal percussion on key words accompanied by simple bordun.
7. Expand the "single cell" form into a rondo form by adding contrasting sections where the children sing something they have planted. The teacher could accompany this with an open harmony to help keep the key-center. Return to the song after two or three children have sung their "plantings". A movement might be added to the song, hinging on the key words plant, rot, grow, pigeon, crow.

A kindergarten in Upper Nyack, N.Y. played with this and came up with this version:

36. Games for Physical Co-ordination and Body Movement

1. "Touch Down"

Play this variation of "Ring-a-Rosie" with a small group of children around a hoop or a rope circle. At "touch down" the body part named is touched to the floor inside the ring.

"Ring around the rosie,
pocket full of posie,
nose, nose, nose touch down!"
(ears, elbows, head, thumbs, etc.)

2. "Oliver Twist" (traditional)

This game may become cumulative by repeating in reverse order each body part named in consecutive verses, ending with "nose . . . toes . . . goes." In this way the game may be a challenge to memory.

"Oliver twist, twist, twist,
(stretch arms over head and twist body)
you can't do this, this, this:
(clap three times)
touch your nose, nose, nose,
touch your toes, toes, toes
and around he goes, goes, goes."
(turn around once in place)

Repeat and add:

"Oliver twist, twist, twist,
you can't do this, this, this:
touch your chin, chin, chin,
touch your nose, nose, nose,
touch your toes, toes, toes," etc.

3. "Mr Knickerbocker"

Clap and move to the beat freely about the room or in a circle.

Hey, Mr Knickerbocker, boppity bop,
you look so good in your boppity bop.
Let's put the music in our feet, feet.
Now we got the music in our feet, feet.

Repeat:

Hey, Mr Knickerbocker, boppity bop,
you look so good in your boppity bop.
Let's put the music in our ....
Now we got the music in our ....

(Children suggest other places to "put the music".)

37. Seven-and-a-Half-Jumps

☐ to react to sound and silence and musical cues

☐ to show tempo and dynamic changes with the body

☐ to increase listening acuity

While hearing a simplified version of the folk-dance tune "Seven Jumps", the children move anywhere in the room, stopping and holding position ("freeze") when the melody stops. After a single "get-ready" tone, a chord is played and the children touch one body part to the floor. This continues cumulatively each time the melody is played, until the children are flat on the floor.

The melody should be played on piano or recorder so that the teacher can vary the pace, tempo and dynamics, and key. Eventually, surprises like stopping after only a phrase, or abrupt changes in tempo, or announcements of a new body part, e.g. right thumb, can be incorporated.

A sample progression might be: one knee, two knees, one elbow, two elbows, forehead, toes, etc. (making the last one a triumphant "belly button!" is enjoyed by the children). Follow with a quiet game on the floor.

38. Sound Story

Make a sound picture after a walk in the park, or after a story has been invented.

Example

A steady or intermittent low tone on an instrument is a squirrel walking along in the grass searching for food, while a scale pattern in a rising sequence sends him up a tree. There a high tremolo has him nibbling an acorn, while a descending scale brings him down again. Other sounds can be found for sleeping curled up in his tree nest, digging a hole to bury nuts or quivering his tail as he takes food from a human hand. (Much will depend on the children's sharpness of observation.)

Whenever possible, the children should choose the sounds, and play them. When all are fixed, the story can be told without words, or a child can tell the story in any sequence he chooses, and the instruments respond on cue. A few children could devise movements, or anyone not playing could pantomime the story.

Extend this to make sound pictures of the children's pets or animals seen at the zoo, or birds.

39. Sound Signs—1

- ☐ Ask the children to play these signs. Let them find their own way to do it. During this process the children will discover that the distance between the signs means time. Problems occur when many children play at the same time—because the time structure is relative.
- ☐ Use this notation as a task in discrimination—the teacher plays one of the examples and children must find which one.
- ☐ Encourage the children to draw their own examples.
- ☐ Different signs here lead to a differentiation in dynamics, and/or instrumentation.

These signs have been printed with a potato. Have the children make their own examples for playing.

PART 2

Instrumental playing begins with a variety of pitched and non-pitched instruments. The teacher introduces this work from entire body movement, through sound gestures to instrumental playing. Much discipline is required because of the necessity to control the energetic outbursts of the children.

Speaking and singing are closely related means of communication in the child's world. Rhythmic speech—which may be high or low in pitch, loud, soft, happy, sad, fast or slow—when combined with movement or an accompaniment may lead to the invention of a melody or to improvised singing. The teacher should include many traditional rhymes and songs as well as new ones. There are many sources for such material which can be developed with the children in a similar way. The melodic range is extended to include the following tonal combinations:

do′-so-do
do′-so-fa-mi-re-do
do′-la-so-mi-re-do
la-so-fa-mi-re-do
la-so-fa-mi-re
do′-la-so-fa-mi-re
mi-re-do-ti-la

There are two songs in which notes without stems are used. In these examples the duration of the notes are not in any fixed meter. They represent the natural flow of the language.

Reading and writing music continues. The children will be finding their own ways to transpose sounds into signs. Such exercises help to develop an understanding for the necessity of musical notation and for its basic principles.

40. Mary Ann

Words from The Puffin Book of Nursery Rhymes

41. Musical "Simon Says"

A game for pitch discrimination

The teacher starts a roll on the lowest temple block. This roll continues throughout the game. The teacher then gives movement instructions to the children: sit down, put your hands on your knees, etc. The children, however, are not to follow the instruction until the teacher plays one of the higher temple blocks once, immediately returning to the roll. The teacher, of course, varies the length of waiting time before playing the higher block, trying to "trick" the children. Usually, no formal rules concerning being "out" are necessary.

42. Giants

- ☐ Invent a melody
- ☐ Make up another piece about elves with the children

43. Cock Robin's Roundelay

Children imitate Robin's "singing". The sound of a triangle signals the end of the improvisation.

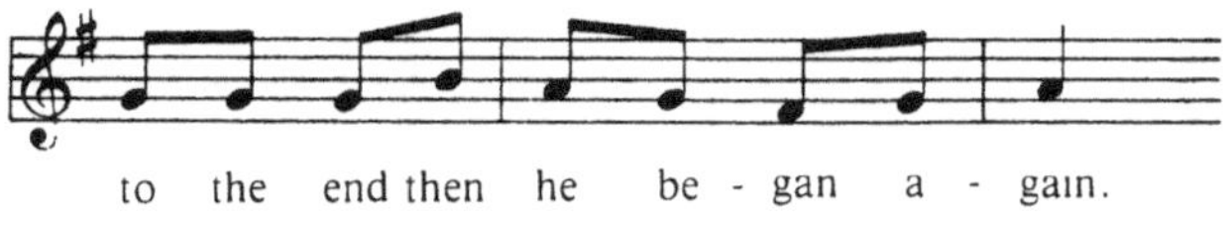

Robin is "singing" again.

Other animals also get up early. They too can sing a roundelay.

Cat Blackfur got up early . . .
Dog Floppy-ears got up early . . .
Sheep Softwool got up early . . .

Prepare a tape with the voices of animals. The children should differentiate the voices, name them and describe them. (Cats do not only meow, they also purr. There are different sized dogs with voices to match!) Create dramatic scenes with the sounds of different animals, e.g. birds sing and chirp . . . a dog barks . . . silence . . . slowly the birds begin to sing again.

44. "Magic Sticks"

1. Teacher and class sit on the floor in Indian fashion. Teacher asks a question and plays the rhythm of the words on a pair of sticks.

   "How are you today?"

   As children give various answers, the teacher echoes each one and plays the rhythm on the sticks, e.g.,

   "I feel terrible" "I'm fine" "I'm sleepy"
   "I have a new tooth" "Just great" "My arm hurts"

   The teacher then suggests that questions and answers be played without words. The magic sticks will do the "talking".

2. Teacher plays a one-measure rhythm on the sticks to each child in the circle. Another pair of sticks is passed from child to child for individual responses. Use floor sounds too.

   Teacher

   Child

   creates answer on "magic sticks" and passes them to the next child.

   or

   or

   or

Suggest that answers be loud and angry, soft, shy, playful or surprised. This encourages listening to the mood and quality of each question and response.

45. Row Your Boat

- ☐ to show a feeling for accent and pulse with the whole body
- ☐ to develop a relationship with a partner and small group

Sing the song often, with the children rocking in place to feel the pulse. When they know it well, they sit facing a partner, grasp both hands and pull back and forth on the accents. The legs may be folded or opened wide, as the children wish.

A story may be improvised about a boat that was too big for one to row across the river, so we must add another person, sitting behind the first . . . still too big, add another, etc, until four are rowing, one behind the other. Conversely, another time, four begin to row, but the boat won't move; one waits for a new boat, etc.

This variation requires a great deal of co-operation and inter-action.

46. Pass the Pattern

- ☐ to reinforce a steady pulse
- ☐ to sharpen perception of patterns
- ☐ to develop co-ordination in repeating rythmic patterns

Formation: Teacher and children in a seated circle.
Each child has a small percussion instrument, either real (sticks, wood block, small drum, finger cymbals) or improvised or made by the children (small box tapped with a mallet, two stones, or coffee-can drum).* The teacher has a larger drum or contrasting-sounding instrument.

After an experimental "go-around" to hear the sound of each instrument individually, or some games which identify the various sounds according to their materials or manner of playing, play the following echo game.

The teacher plays a short pattern on her drum, perhaps  and each child in turn tries to repeat it without error. This is "Pass the Pattern" and should progress around the circle without pause, comment, or correction. Some children can retain and repeat the pattern even when the one before him has not played it properly. Eventually extend these patterns to 3/4 and 6/8 time.

Preparation for this game may be done with clapping and patsching, with a line of a poem spoken rhythmically, or in movement with simple arm and leg and head gestures. The teacher should move to another part of the circle when the game is repeated to give several children a chance to be first to receive the pattern, especially in a group of more than ten children.

Avoid instruments that give a double or clouded sound, such as maracas, jingles or bells.

47. Body Letters

Lying on the floor, the children put their bodies into shapes suggested by the teacher: an airplane, a turtle, a chair, a cup. (Some shapes may need two children.) Extend this by having the children form letters of the alphabet with their bodies. The children will discover that some letters are easier to shape than others, and some may require two or more children.

Variation: One child can help his partner make the shape or the letter, and then they trade places.

48. Ducks in the Millpond

1. Introduce language phrases through echo clapping and speaking.
2. Establish this pattern of sound gestures;
   4 snaps, 4 claps, 4 patsching sounds, 3 stamps.
3. Add language patterns to this accompaniment.
4. Transfer sound accompaniment to unpitched percussion.
5. Add movement game with language or song.

Game

1. Form; Circle of children around the "millpond" . . . hands on hips. Two children in center are the ducks.
2. In imitation of the duck walk, children take four walking steps on "ducks in the millpond." Circle moves left.
3. Jump toward center of circle and touch floor on "fell in the millpond."
4. Stand and shake arms on "wet all over."
5. Stretch up and repeat sound gestures for chorus.

(During chorus the two children in the middle skip in and out of the millpond and stop in front of the person they come to on the last word of the chorus. These two children now go to the center.)

49. Follow Me

☐ Teacher and children join hands to form line. Play "Follow the Leader." This can lead to formation of circle or other shapes, straight line, serpent line, etc.

☐ As children sit in circle, take turns being leader to start non-locomotor motion that others follow. Try to continue the song without stopping from one leader to the next. Successive leaders can decide on their motion during the first phrase of the song with all joining in by the second phrase.

50. Games with Hula-Hoops

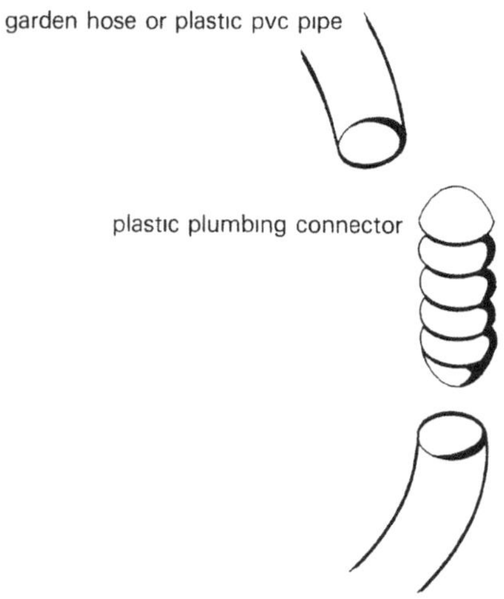

☐ to react to sound using a "prop"

☐ to increase awareness of space

☐ to move while chanting or singing

(If hula-hoops are unavailable at toy stores, they may be made with plastic pipe connectors of the proper size and lengths of garden hose about 1 ½ meters long.)

1. Each child stands inside his hoop and holds it at waist level with arms outstretched. This is his "car" and he must drive it slowly and carefully in the traffic in the room. Small instruments may be assigned to be signals for traffic lights, or other children may like to be the policeman, crossing guard or gas station attendant. A poem or song about cars, such as Woody Guthrie's "Take me riding in the Car" (Folkways Album, "Songs to Grow On," Vol.1) may be sung as an interlude. Eventually sound signals for a straight super-highway, curving country road, steep hill, etc, may be added, and the children should be encouraged to improvise.

2. Three or four hula-hoops are placed on the floor, widely separated. These are puddles and may be splashed in freely while a poem about the rain is chanted or a song sung. Precisely on the last word, all must be out of the puddles, drying their feet.

Some examples of rhymes

Rain on the green grass,
rain on the tree,
rain on the rooftops,
but not on me!

Doctor Foster went to Gloucester
in a shower of rain.
He stepped in a puddle,
up to his middle,
and never went there again.

3. Several hoops are laid out close together in a line on the floor, and each child tries to step through them all in sequence. At first, two feet will rest in each hoop, but with practice, an alternating-foot trot may develop. A partner for each child might play a soft timpani pulse to assist this.

Variation: After some experience, set up a pattern of hoops and spaces and let the children try to say the pattern as they step it: "step, step, jump, rest", etc.

51. Hickory Dickory Dock

- ☐ to react quickly to sounds and silence
- ☐ to reinforce good understanding of pulse by playing instruments

A circle of children, standing, sings the song while one walks around the outside (on tiptoe) as the mouse. Two children in the center play a two-toned wood block for the clock, and a triangle for the chime. At the chime of "one", the mouse taps someone, who immediately begins to chase him, aiming for that empty space. The one left without a space becomes the next mouse, while the former one goes to the center to play an instrument.

Should this prove too exciting, and the children shout encouragement rather than sing the last phrase, the tapping and running may be held off until the last phrase of the song.

Variation: In the beginning, a quieter game may be devised, with the children swaying arms or shifting weight on the legs on ♩. ♩. accent. The mouse merely chooses another to take his place at "one".

52. Three Folk Rhymes

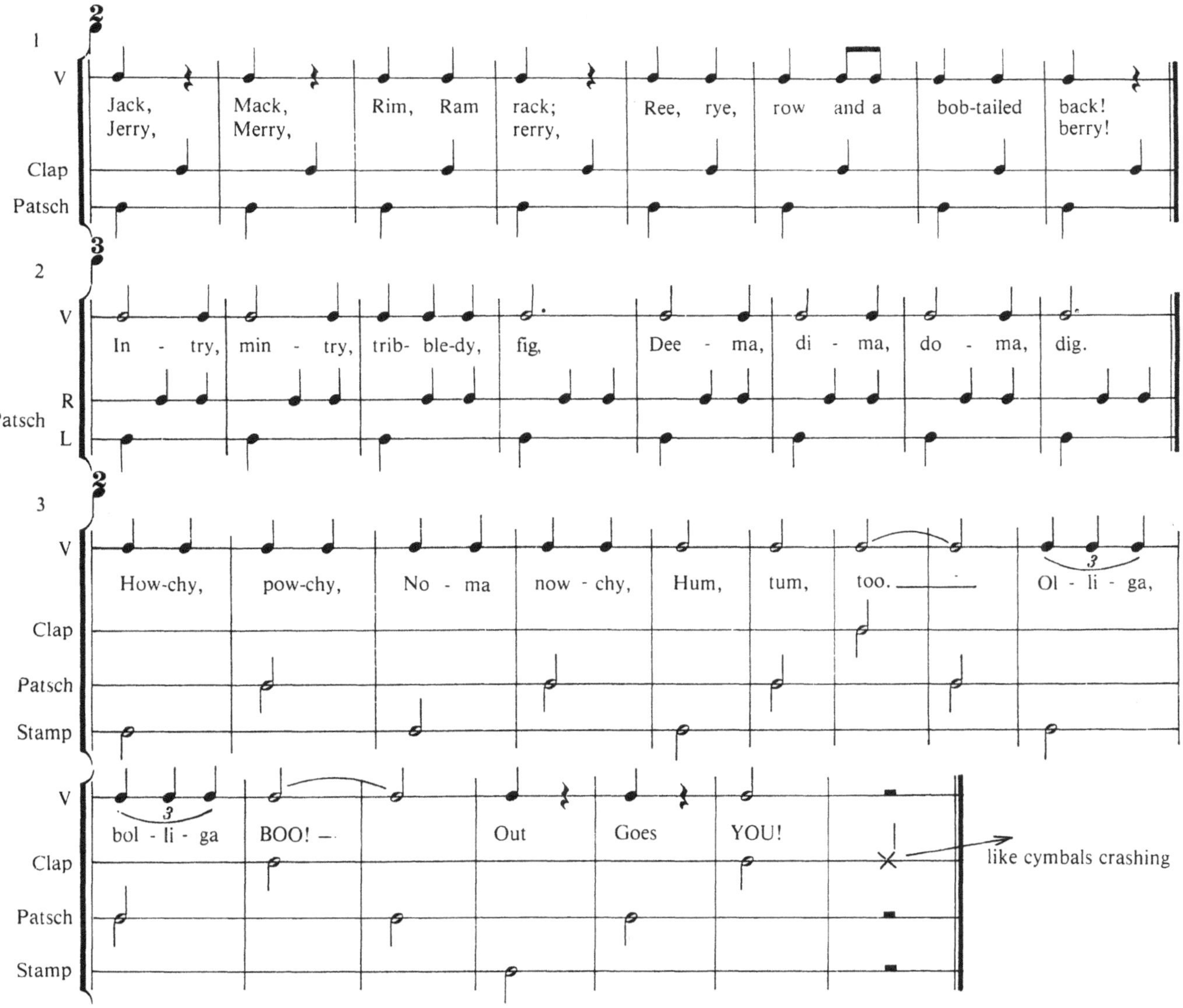

53. Lemonade

(an old game, simpler than charades, which serves as an early experience in pantomime)

Children divide into two groups, parallel lines facing each other.
Group One decides secretly what motion they will pantomime for Group Two to guess.
Group One, in line, approaches Group Two:

One: Here we come.
Two: Where you from?
One: New York.
Two: What's your trade?
One: Lemonade.
Two: Get to work and show us something if you're not afraid.

All members of Group One then begin to pantomime (e.g. throwing a ball, playing jacks, jumping rope, pushing a swing, sweeping, etc.)
If Group Two guesses correctly, all of Group One runs back to home base, trying not to be tagged by any member of Group Two. Those who *are* tagged must join the other group.
If Group Two has made three incorrect guesses, Group One tells them the answer and makes up a new pantomime action. Then Group Two has a turn . . .

The same game may also be played without tag; or with one child pantomiming and the group guessing or with the children, in parallel lines as above, but each child has a partner – one to pantomime and one to guess.

54. Lullaby "Taa, Taa, Yee"

This song is a lullaby from Ghana. The untranslated words have no specific meaning but are meant to be words of comfort. "Taa, taa-tee, yee, yee, yee" are "patting" words. "Yaa, ya-Awusi-o" sung to quiet the crying child might be our equivalent of "shh". African children learn very soon to clap and stamp these complex rhythms which would be far too difficult for very young American children. The rhythm patterns are included here only to give an idea how African children accompany their own singing.

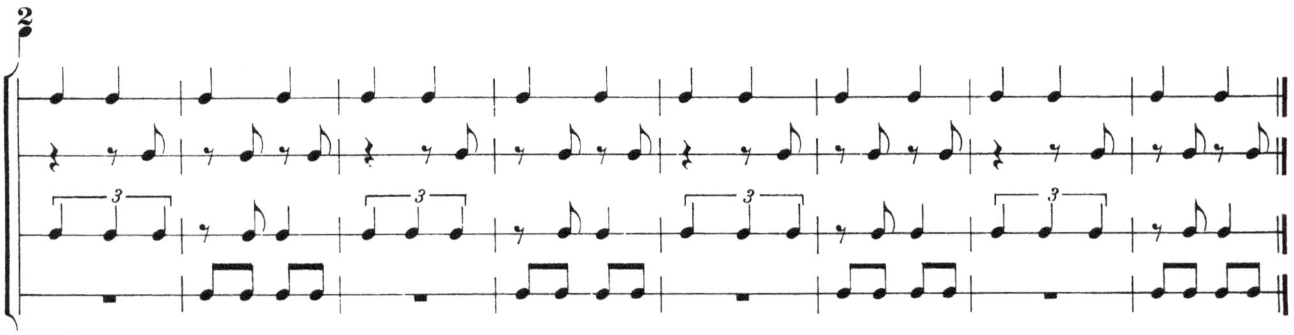

Taa, taa, tee,
yee, yee, yee,
Kaafo ama.
Yaa, ya A-wusi o.

Taa, taa, tee,
Yee, yee, yee,
Don't cry.
Yaa, ya-Awusi o.

from: African Songs and Rhythms for Children, *a selection from Ghana by W. K. Amoaku, Schott Ed. 6376. Folkways Record FC 7844 (recorded and annotated by Dr. W. K. Amoaku – Orff-Schulwerk in the African Tradition, 1978.*

55. The Children Walk

1. The children walk, without bumping into each other, freely about the room. Each child walks at his own pace and accompanies each step with a clap. At the request of the teacher, the children come to a common pulse. The teacher then plays on a hand-drum the pulse arrived at by the children. The children stop clapping, but continue to walk, matching their steps with the drum. When the drum stops, they stop or otherwise react in a predetermined way (sit, kneel, balance on the right foot, touch the color blue, etc.).

2. The children, individually, walk a designated pathway on the floor (e.g. ∞ ∼ Z) to the pulse of a hand-drum played by the teacher. At the cessation of the music, they make the same pathway in the air, using one hand or both hands clasped together. Different levels may be used and the space in front, in back, and to the sides of the body explored.

3. The children walk freely throughout the room to the pulse of the hand-drum played by the teacher. At the cessation of the pulse, the children freeze. They clap the pulse of the rhythmic improvisation played by the teacher on the wood rim of the hand-drum. When the teacher resumes playing the pulse on the skin of the hand-drum, the children resume walking. Different tempi may be used for the pulse and rhythm sections.

56. Music Pictures – 1

- ☐ to encourage improvisation with simple forms
- ☐ to develop ear-eye-hand co-ordination
- ☐ to increase awareness of relative pitches

Seated in a circle, each one takes a turn to make a gesture in the air that matches the sound he is making: e.g. slow rise and curved fall of the arm to show a siren. This is immediately imitated by the others.

Possible progression and/or variations:

Extend the gestures by using the whole body to "draw" the designs in the air, beginning perhaps with two children facing each other and trying out each others' patterns.

Let one or two children at a time continue a favorite sound and gesture with chalk in hand(s) at the blackboard, followed by the class "reading" the design and doing it.

Help the children discover the many kinds of lines and colors to be obtained with the side of the chalk: what sound and gesture goes with a thin line? a series of broad dashes? wiggly lines?

When a few designs are on the board, let the children decide on the order in which they will be sounded and moved to. A simple form like A B A may emerge. Someone might point to and "draw" the shapes with a pointer or mallet handle while the others do it. Experiment with different tempi.

Extend this another time by letting the children draw on large pieces of paper with chalk. Pin them around the room and have the children make a composition by altering the sequence.

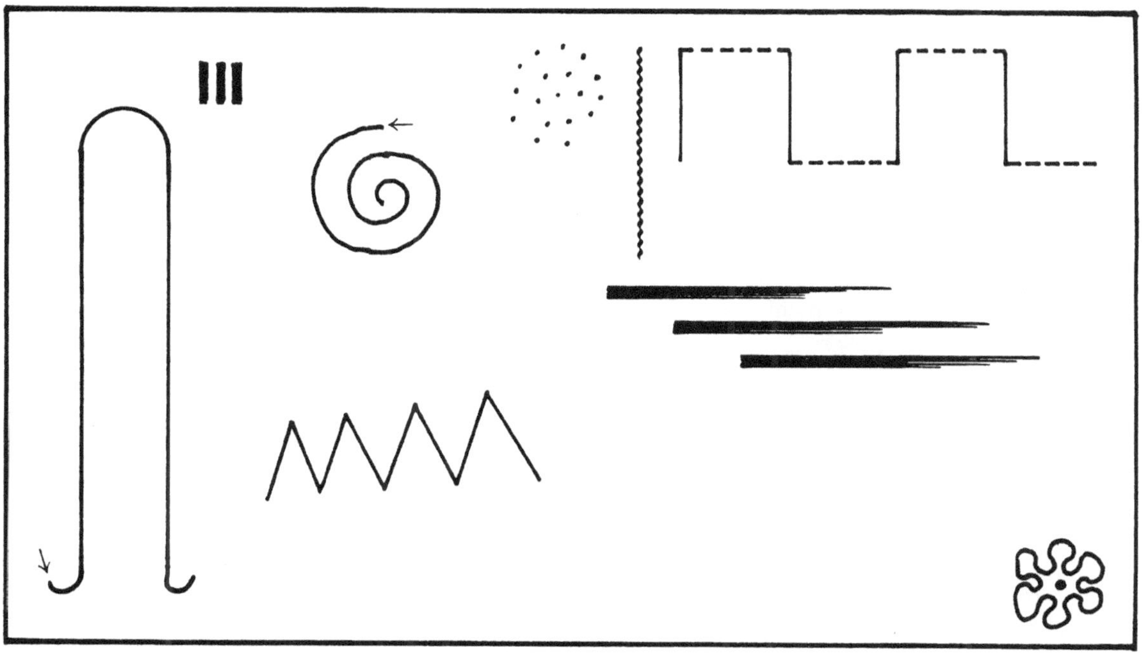

57. Gregory Griggs

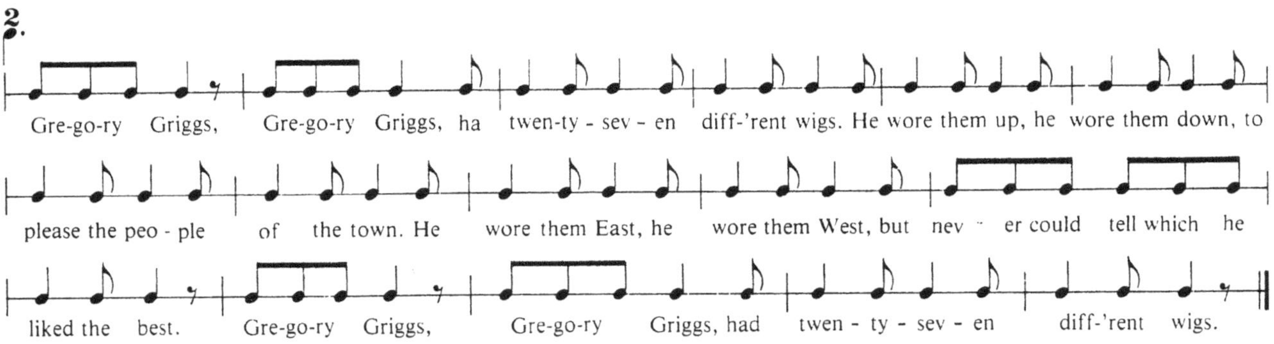

Suggestion: Have the children patsch on each "Gregory Griggs", and clap on "up", "down", "East" and "West".

For a more elaborate setting of this rhyme see Richard Gill, Have You Any Wool? Three Bags Full! *(Orff Schulwerk American Edition Supplement).*

58. Water Sounds

Recalling their first hand experiences, class and teacher discuss household "water" sounds: dripping faucet, glass filling up, pouring out of a small-necked bottle, bathtub, shower, washing machine, garden hose, etc. The children try to show these varied speeds and intensities in movement. Later, some could try to find instruments to accompany the groups for each one.

If possible, extend this to country sounds: a little spring, rain dripping from trees, river, waterfall, a bubbling creek, snow melting, icicles, etc.

"Live" demonstrations and experiments in the classroom, with an eyedropper, two pitchers and at the wash-up sink will reinforce these concepts and contrasts.

Ask the children to listen to a tape with the sounds of water

a) slowly dripping
b) running fast
c) producing a high pitched sound
d) producing a low pitched sound

Let the children talk about their observations.

59. Hunt the Cows

A section: Children jump up and down in time to the music.
B section: 1st phrase — kneel on one knee
2nd phrase — kneel on both knees
3rd phrase — one elbow on the floor
4th phrase — both elbows on the floor

With each repitition, the A section becomes faster, the B section slower. Start out in a moderate tempo. Children love jumping up at the end to sing the A section.

60. Counting Rhyme

One for the money,
two for the show,
three to make ready,
and four to go.

Experiment with different word-rhythms.
Include word-rhythms discovered by the children.

Examples

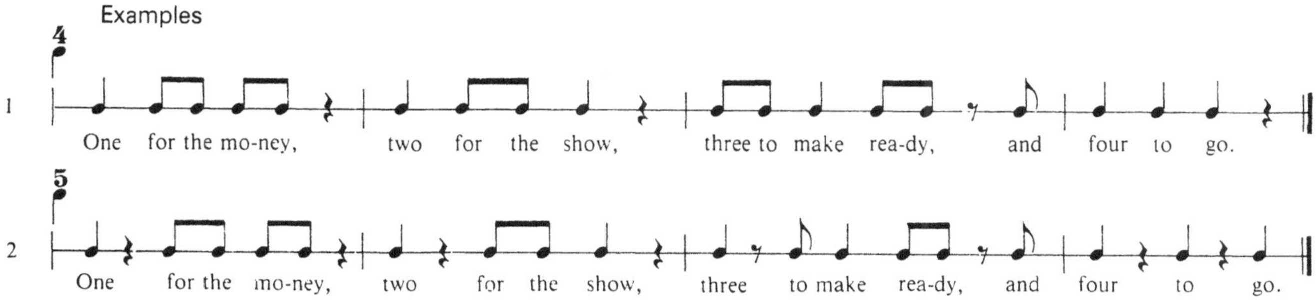

61. Corn Grinding Song

Stone-passing Game to play while singing

1. Equipment: a set of smooth stones, one of which is painted with bright designs.

2. Formation: players in circle, sitting close together. Each player has a stone in front of him.

3. Each child in rhythm picks up stone, placing it on floor in front of the child on the right. This movement is done throughout the song.

4. At the end of the song, child with the painted stone in front of him is eliminated (i.e. he joins the musicians' circle choosing bells, rattles or sticks to play).

Simple version of game:

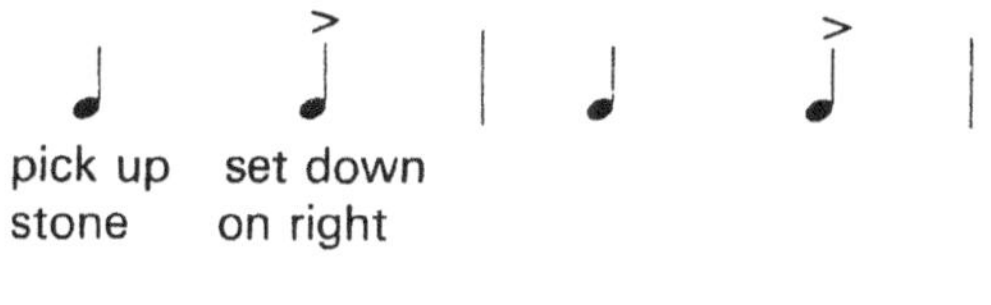

Advanced version:

Note: Flute interlude is eliminated when using the song for this game.

This game version from Dance down the Rain, Sing up the Corn, *R. and E. Research Associates, San Francisco. Used by permission*

62. A Candle Suite

He's (She's) standing like a candle,
he's (she's) melted quite enough.
First we'll go gently,
then we'll blow tough! (*Puff!*)

The children stand in a circle while one child, standing in the center, imitates the candle. The children sing "Jeremiah, blow the fire", walking around the candle. As they sing, "Puff, puff, puff", they face the center, hands on hips, and attempt to blow out the candle. The instrumental parts can be prepared by walking slowly, then quickly, associating the duration of quarter and half notes with the words of the song.

"Jack be nimble" is accompanied with a simple partner game. While in the circle, turn to face a neighbour. Pat the knees and then partner's hands while speaking the rhyme. The center child hops or skips around the inside of the circle, jumping to the center at the appropriate time.

The third poem is an opportunity for the center child to be the focus of attention. As the children speak, the candle "melts" and is finally blown out. If the song is repeated at this point, the center child may walk around the inside of the circle, choosing a new candle.

Each of these sections should be introduced in different lessons. When each section is learned the children can be encouraged to design their own larger form. They may choose to use all three parts in succession, make a rondo form, or perform a simple three-part form.

63. Old Jeremiah

Old Jeremiah,
he jumped in the fire.
The fire was so hot
he jumped in the pot.
The pot was so black
he jumped in the crack.
The crack was so high
he jumped in the sky.
The sky was so blue
he jumped in the canoe.
The canoe was so shallow
he jumped in the tallow.
The tallow was so soft
he jumped in the loft.
The loft was so rotten
he jumped in the cotton.
The cotton was so white
that there he concluded to stay all night.

64. Jack be Nimble

- ☐ to be able to react to the precise end of the song
- ☐ to understand the relationship of time and space and to adjust steps accordingly

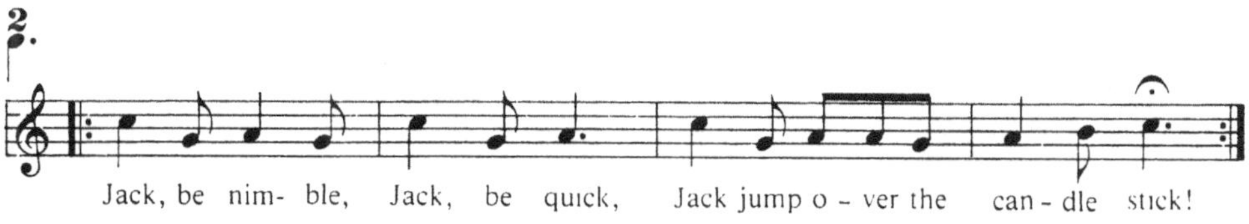

The children place their separate shoes anywhere on the floor, spacing them out as evenly as possible. The traditional rhyme is chanted or sung as the children skip around and between the shoes. On the last word ("stick") each child jumps over the shoe nearest him at the moment. If it is his, he sits down and puts it on, and the game continues around him. Should this prove difficult in a small room, the child merely picks up the shoe and carries it with him until he finds the other one. Then he takes both to one side and puts them on.

See Speech Exercise, Volume 2, No. 105, p. 74, and setting by R. Gill in the supplement Have You Any Wool? Three Bags Full, *Schott Music Corp.*

65. Sound Signs—2

These signs shall represent the sounds of different instruments. Have the children find a variety of ways in which to play them. Talk about and try out different ways to translate these signs into sounds. There is no right or wrong.

1.
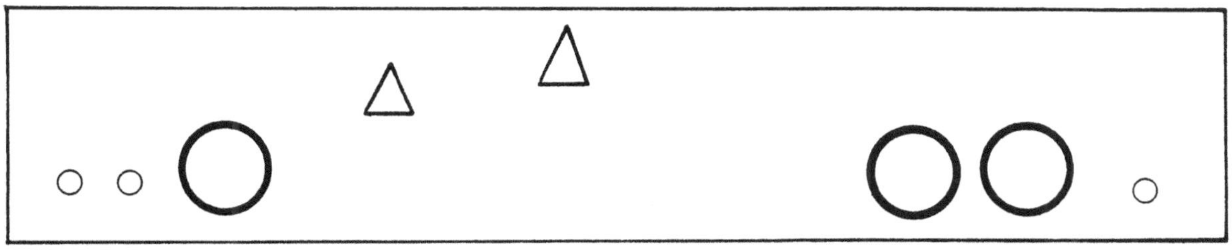

2.
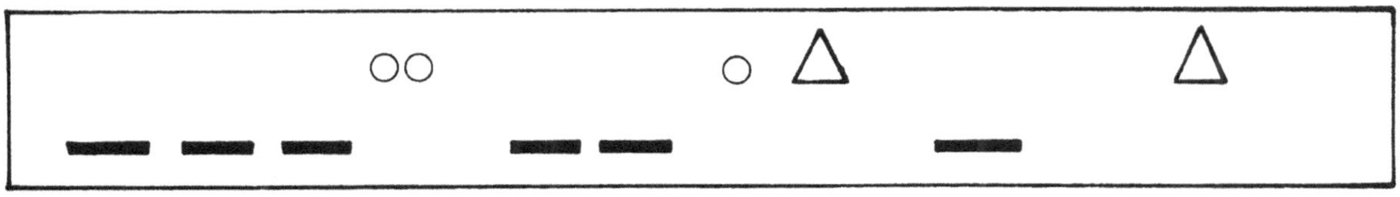

3.
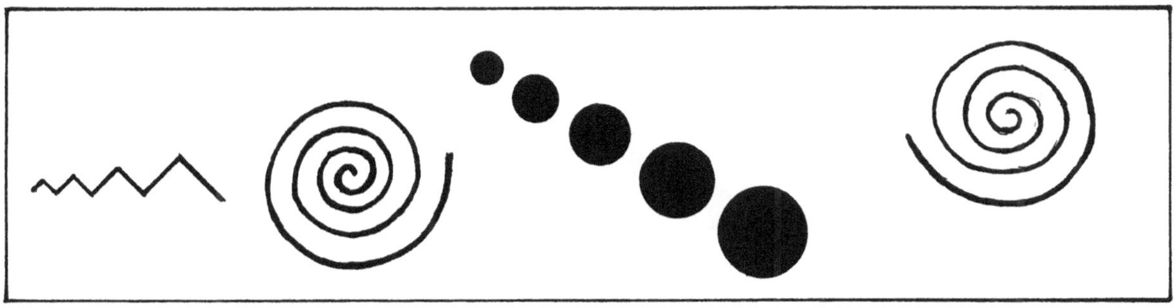

4.

66. There was an Owl

Words The Puffin Book of Nursery Rhymes, *Iona and Peter Opie, Penguin Books Ltd, Harmondsworth, Engl. pg. 35.*

67. Easter Eggs

- ☐ to reinforce pulse through speaking in rhythm
- ☐ to stimulate the imagination
- ☐ to co-ordinate sound gestures with speaking

The children are seated in a circle with the teacher. All chant the "chorus" together:

"An egg, an egg, what kind of egg?"

Each child in turn, goind around the circle, names a kind of egg and chants it, trying to keep the pulse. The rest of the class repeats it immediately.

Example: "A soft-boiled egg"
"A scrambled egg"

"A goose egg"

Any child who cannot think of anything should be encouraged to say "Easter Egg" so as not to feel embarrassed at losing a turn or causing a pause in the rhythm.

Eventually this can be extended by accompanying the speaking with a soft, alternating patsch on each knee.

NB. This game can also be an introduction to the anacrusis.

68. Lou Pripet (The Carpet Maker)

The traditional accompaniment for this dance is played by one person with a one-hand flute and drum.

Dance Form

Formation

A circle in which the children are standing very close together with hands joined.

Steps

[A] moving counter-clockwise starting with left foot with one step per ♩ beat. Arms swing in and out, starting in

[B] in place, facing center, leaning slightly backward with arms stretched horizontally forward, "scissors kick" in following rhythm: the "kicking" is stretched forward.

Suggestions for development

1. Play the tune and let the children move freely while listening to distinguish parts [A] and [B]. This can be made clear by adding the ♫♩ accompaniment to [B] or playing the melody an octave higher, etc.
2. Let the children join in with ♫♩ rhythm of the [B] section with sound gestures they choose themselves. ([A]: move around freely, [B]: in place)

   All sing the melody. (Perhaps you would like to invent some words of your own..?) [A]: walk in place, [B]: children take turns showing their sound gesture/movement patterns while the others imitate. Children enjoy doing this activity kneeling, sitting or lying down, playing the ♫♩ rhythm with feet or hands on the floor.
4. [A]: swing arms in and out

   [B]: light stamps in place, Let children experiment with free leg: knees lifted high, free leg thrown backward, to the side or forward, etc.
5. Dance the original form. You can make the circle gradually bigger (B_1) and small again (B_2).

69. One Misty, Moisty Morning

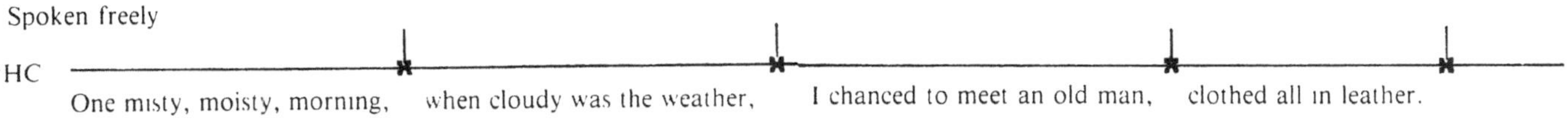

1. Teacher speaks part 1 freely while improvising sound on metallophone. Children repeat language with sound accompaniment.

2. Teacher speaks part 2 emphasizing the difference in feeling. Children speak part 2 while clapping pulse.
3. Children explore the feeling of moving through space in a "misty, moisty" way, while speaking part 1, and walking briskly with drum beat during part 2.
4. Add game and give accompaniment parts to children.

   Part 1

   Free, creative movements stressing the feeling of the language.

   Part 2

   Children walk freely in tempo. On the three "how do you do?" phrases, they turn to greet a passing child by clapping or shaking hands. After greeting third child, they keep that child as a partner and squat down quickly on the word "again".

Orchestration suggestion:

Metallophones improvise sound for part 1. Cymbal or gong is played at the end of each line.

Part 2: the dotted quarter pulse is played on timpani. Play word rhythms on temple blocks, speaking words silently.

Words from "Mother Goose"

70. Hiding Chant

Bushel of wheat, bushel of rye,
all not hid, holler "Aye!"
(Wait briefly)
Bushel of wheat, bushel of clover,
all not hid can't hide over.
Here I come, ready or not!

(Or substitute this line for last line:
Here I come, both eyes open!)

Simply play this game: don't attempt to "teach" it!

71. Jack and Gill

Find accompanying actions with fingers, hands, arms.

Words A Book of Nonsense, *Edward Lear, Lewis Caroll a.o., edited by Ernest Rhys, An Everyman Paperback, Dent: London ISBN 0 460 01806X.*

72. Happiness

by A. A. Milne

1. Memorize the poem, introducing key sound gestures one at a time. As the children are comfortable stamping on the first two words, add the clapping sounds and repeat several times.
2. When all sound gestures have been introduced, practice speaking the words silently while adding body accompaniments.
3. Transfer sound gestures to unpitched percussion.
   snap = triangle or finger cymbals
   clap = woodblock
   patsch = tambourine
   stamp = drum
4. Perform in the following variations;
   a. language with sound gestures
   b. unpitched percussion alone
   c. all three

73. I Like Coffee

I like coffee, I like tea.
I'd like________to follow me.
(1, 2, 3, 4, 5, 6, 7 𝄽)
(Adapted from a traditional jump rope rhyme)

The children sit in a circle and one child stands in the center. As all the children chant the rhyme the child in the center supplies the name of the child who is invited to the center. The second child imitates or mirrors the movements of the first child. When the chant begins anew, the first child returns to the circle and the second child becomes the leader.

Counting to seven may determine the length of metered movement to be imitated, such as hopping, skipping, or galloping. Silence or soft vocal sounds supplied by the children in the circle may encourage unmetered, mirrored movement. Help the children to realise that the leader is responsible for creating movement that can be understood and imitated by his classmates. This is when the game is fun for everyone.

74. Three Wise Men of Gotham

Words from Edward Lear, Lewis Carroll and others, A Book of Nonsense *edited by Ernest Rhys, Everyman's Library, Dutton, New York, pg. 153.*

75. Introducing the Hand Drum

After passing out the hand drums, allow the children to experiment freely with making sounds. Anything goes as long as the drum is not abused. Show children from the beginning that when not in use, a hand drum should be laid *skin down* on the floor. Children may also use drums as play props: steering-wheels, etc. At a given signal children lay drums down.

Children play "Follow the leader," each child leading in showing a sound or use of the drum he has found.

The teacher takes a turn as leader, using any ametrical sounds which the children may not have thought of. They should include playing at various tempi, using various parts of the body to scrape, pat, tap or rub various parts of the drum, or speaking into the drum. Merely picking a number of drums off the floor quickly at the same time makes an interesting sound. Also have children play at voice commands; e.g. play something soft, something fast. The teacher may also intersperse some metrical playing, such as a pulse or simple ostinato, such as ♫♩ or ♩♩♫♩. For this it is easiest to have children put the drums on their laps with the skin turned to the dominant hand.

Ask the children what the sounds they have made remind them of. Most likely you will get a collection of ideas out of which you can tell an improvised story, perhaps about a parade, or about a rain storm. As you tell the story, the children provide appropriate sound effects.

If you wish to spend more time on listening skills, you could have a child make a sound on his hand drum while the others have their eyes closed. The other children would try to duplicate the kind of sound exactly.

76. Dynamics

Unvoiced sounds are effective means for practicing dynamic changes of loud and soft. (When the full voice is used, children often mistake a high pitch for loud and a low pitch for soft.) The following exercises can use the sound of **s, sh, ch, f,** or **wh,** sounded continuously. In fact, any voiceless sounds of wind or waves that the children can provide are useful.

1) The teacher, later a child, leads dynamic change using the hands horizontally—the distance indicating degree of loudness.

2) The children are encouraged to find other ways of "conducting". Such an exercise can become specific: a "wind" piece, perhaps. Such a conducting exercise leads naturally into movement improvisation as well as notation. Together with the children, find various ways of drawing dynamic changes. Such drawing leads to other ways of notating dynamic change ("keep coloring harder and harder," one child said). The teacher, if it is desired, can then explain the dynamic markings used in traditional notation.

77. Sound Signs—3

In these examples the size of the sign represents the dynamic level. Have the children play them on different instruments individually or in groups.

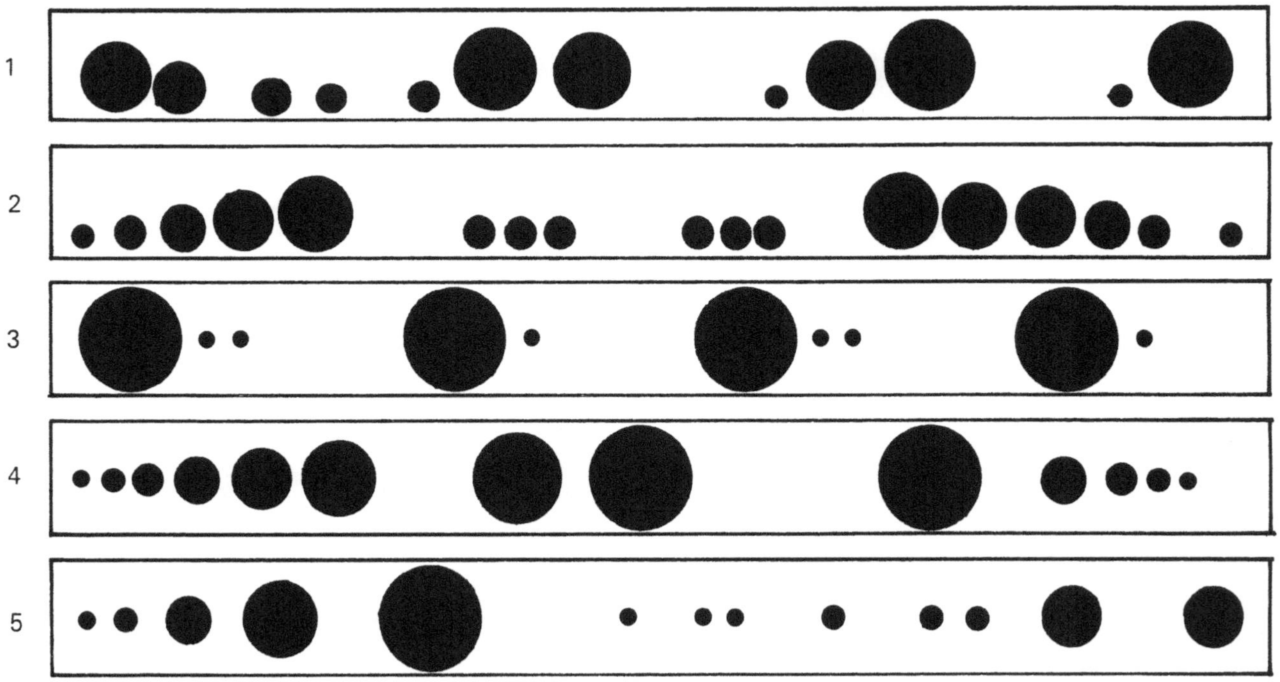

It is not difficult to come from these signs to an understanding of the traditional symbols for crescendo and decrescendo.

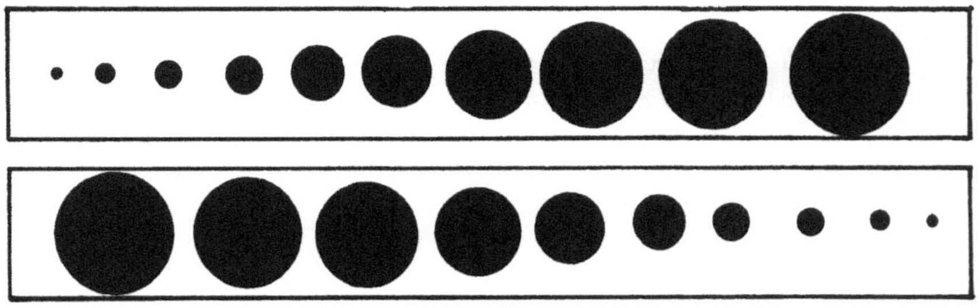

78. Fairies

from the Brothers Grimm

In this piece the following characters take part:

Grouchy mother	ratchet [R]
Grouchy daughter	afuchê, an Afro-American rattle instrument (a gourd with an outer mesh of beads) [A]
Slithering, slimy toads and snakes	maracas (gourd rattles) [M]
Gentle, kind daughter	sand blocks [SaB]
Roses and Jewels	sleigh bells and other small bells [SB/B]
Fairy	finger cymbals (play only one sound each time) [FC]
Prince	bass drum and cymbal [BD/C]

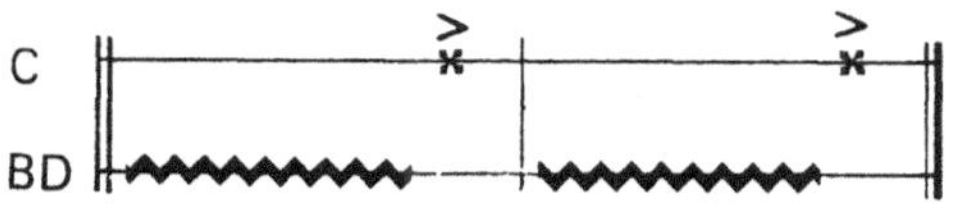

broom	tambourine [Tamb]

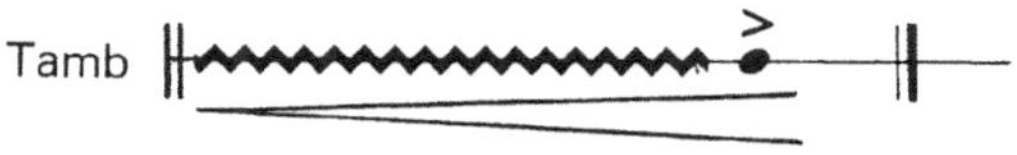

walking to the stream	temple blocks (or wood blocks), tempo as indicated [TB]

The teacher narrates as the children listen and accompany on their instruments.

The introduction and coda can be played from the graphic notation. The children who play must know their parts and perhaps even practice them briefly. The teacher should conduct only if the children cannot make their own entrances as required. After a bit of practice one of the children may be the conductor or the story-teller.

Find other fairy tales appropriate for a similar setting.

Introduction

Play instruments as if in conversation, without interrupting.
Symbols show relative amount of time each instrument plays.

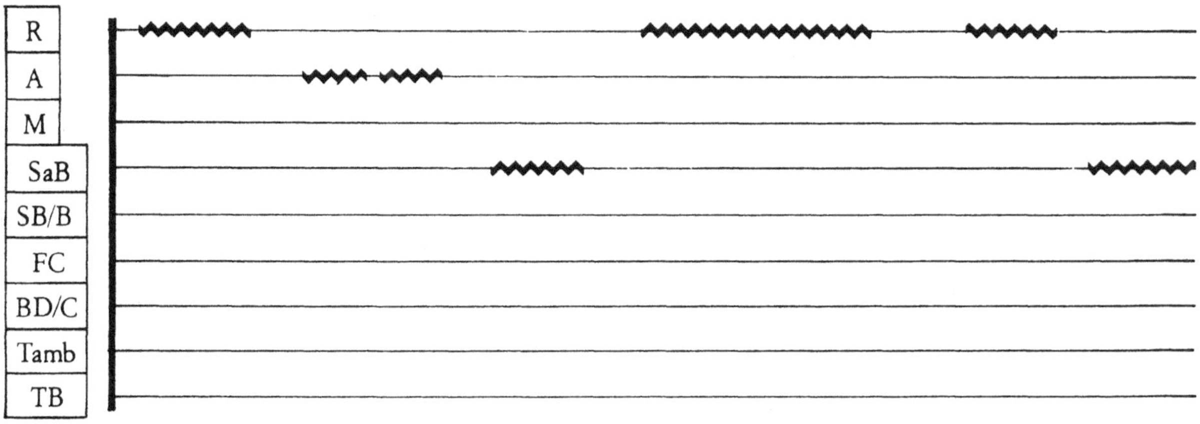

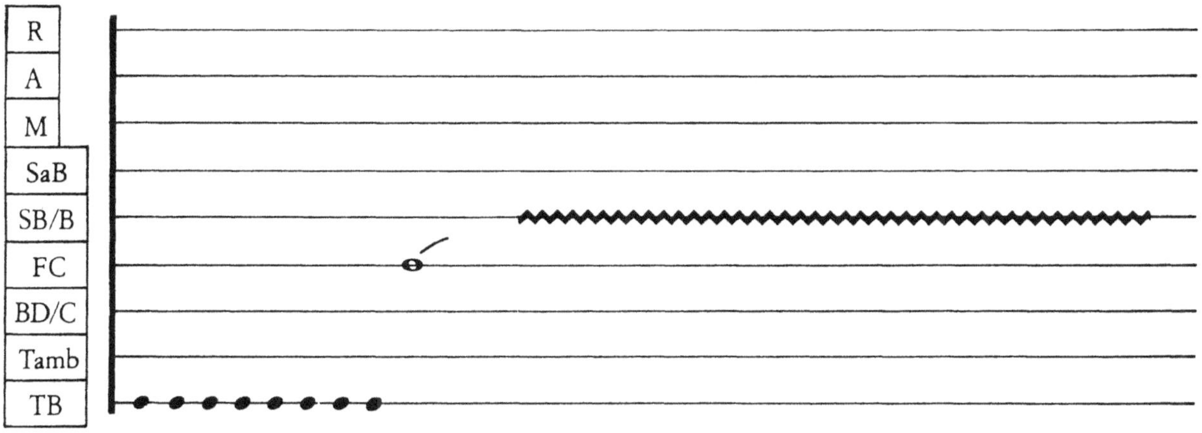

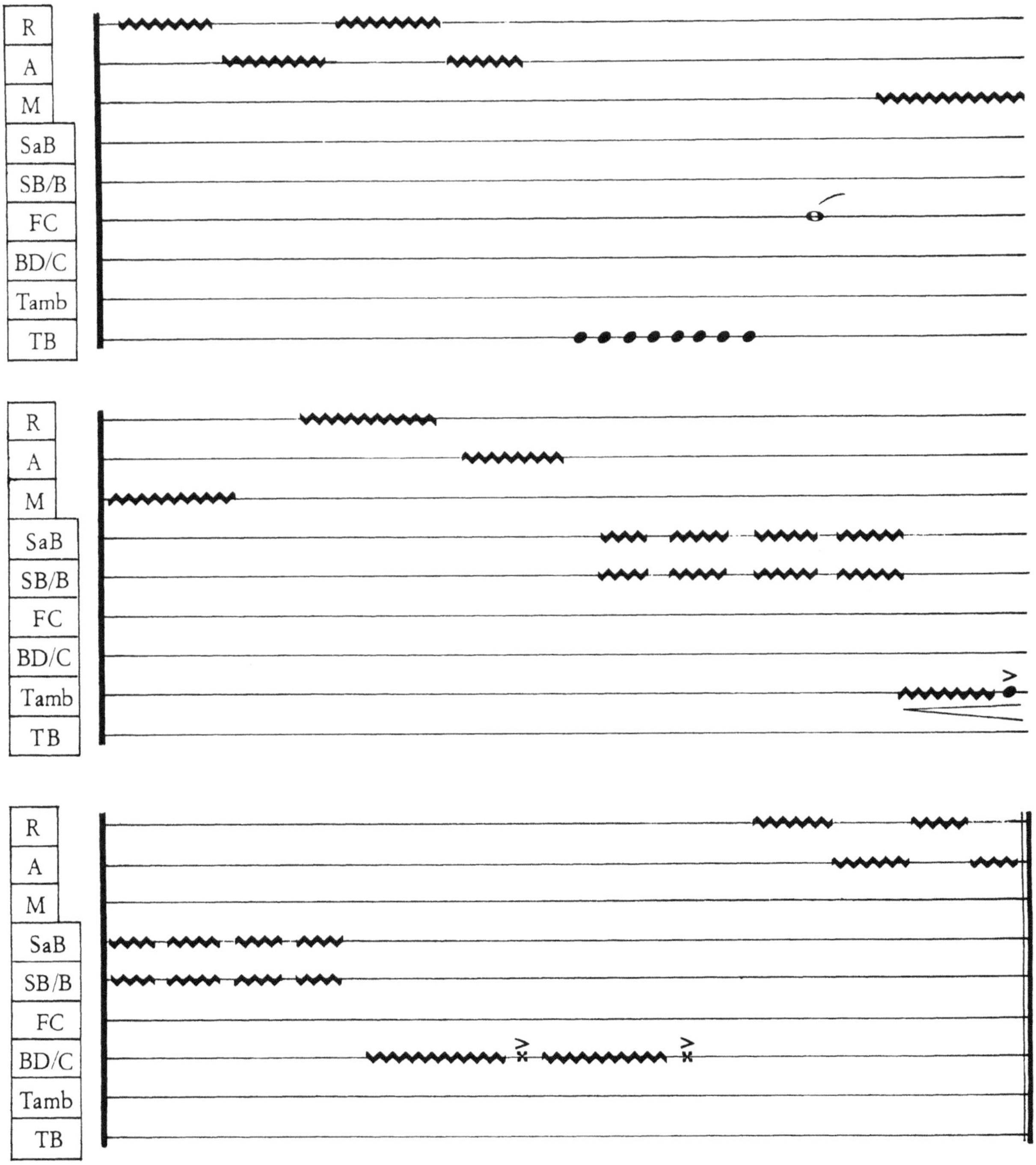

Narrator

Once upon a time there was a very unpleasant, grouchy mother RATCHET who lived with her two daughters in a house on the hill. The elder daughter AFUCHÊ was at least as unpleasant as her mother, but the younger daughter SAND BLOCKS was gentle and kind.

As you might guess, the unpleasant mother RATCHET loved her unpleasant older daughter AFUCHÊ much more than she loved her gentle, kind younger daughter. SAND BLOCKS

Every day, besides doing all the cleaning and cooking and washing, the gentle, kind, younger daughter SAND BLOCKS had to walk a mile down the hill to a stream to fill a pitcher with water, then walk back up the hill to her house. TEMPLE BLOCKS (walk down *moderato,* back up *lento.)*

One day as she was starting back home with her full pitcher, an old, old woman stopped her. FINGER CYMBALS

"May I have a drink of your water?" she asked. FINGER CYMBALS

"Of course you may", replied the gentle and kind younger daughter. SAND BLOCKS And she gave her a drink of water.

FINGER CYMBALS "You are a kind and gentle lady, and I shall reward you." With that, the old, old woman disappeared! FINGER CYMBALS

The kind and gentle younger daughter walked up the hill with her heavy pitcher of water. TEMPLE BLOCKS

RATCHET "Why are you so late?" her unpleasant mother shouted as she came near the house.

"Oh, Mother dear . . . " SAND BLOCKS, SLEIGH BELLS, BELLS and from her mouth came, along with her words, red roses and gleaming white pearls.

RATCHET "You, my dear daughter," she said to her unpleasant older daughter, "shall go to the stream. The old woman is stupid to give such gifts to a goon like your sister. Go, my love, and collect such a reward for your own sweet self."

AFUCHÊ "No!" screamed the unpleasant older daughter, "I won't go! I'm no servant!"

RATCHET "Yes, you will!" shouted her mother.

AFUCHÊ "No, I won't!"

RATCHET "Yes, you will!"

AFUCHÊ "I won't!"

RATCHET "You will!"

She did finally go, slowly, down the hill, TEMPLE BLOCKS carrying only a small cream pitcher to bring back water in.

At the stream she saw not an old, old woman but a well-dressed young lady.

FINGER CYMBALS "May I have a drink of your water?" FINGER CYMBALS

AFUCHÊ "Get your own water. I'll not share mine with you."

FINGER CYMBALS "Then I shall give you a gift to go with your bad manners." FINGER CYMBALS

And the lady disappeared. FINGER CYMBALS

The unpleasant older daughter trudged slowly back up the hill TEMPLE BLOCKS where her mother was waiting most impatiently.

RATCHET "You're so slow! Speak to me!"

AFUCHÊ "It's because . . . " AFUCHÊ, MARACAS And she stopped speaking, horrified, for from her mouth, along with the words, were falling slimy, slippery, slooshy toads and snakes. AFUCHÊ, MARACAS

RATCHET "Aargh! *That's* not what I wanted!" the unpleasant mother said.

RATCHET "It must be all *your* fault," she said to her younger daughter, and she grabbed a broom and chased her daughter from the house. TAMBOURINE

Sadly the kind and gentle younger daughter wandered through the forest and fields. SAND BLOCKS When it began to be dark, she found a large, comfortable tree which she lay down under, and she cried herself to sleep. All night long she dreamed of roses and pearls and lovely things. SLEIGH BELLS, BELLS

LOW DRUM, CYMBAL "What's that?" she cried. SAND BLOCKS She jumped to her feet, surprised that it was morning already, and listened again.

BASS DRUM, CYMBAL Suddenly, over the hill, a handsome prince came riding.

BASS DRUM, CYMBAL "Ah, my dear. What seems to be the trouble? you look as if you've been crying all night."

"Oh, Sire . . . " SAND BLOCKS, SLEIGH BELLS, BELLS

BASS DRUM, CYMBAL "I believe I know," said the prince. "The fairy has rewarded a kind and gentle girl with the gift of speaking with roses and pearls and all manner of lovely things. Come with me to my castle, and we will be very happy." BASS DRUM, CYMBAL

And so the handsome prince and the kind and gentle younger daughter rode off together to the castle where they undoubtedly lived happily ever after. BASS DRUM, CYMBAL, SAND BLOCKS, SLEIGH BELLS, BELLS

Meanwhile, back at the house on the hill, the unpleasant mother and her unpleasant daughter were still shouting at each other.

RATCHET

AFUCHÊ, MARACAS

RATCHET

AFUCHÊ, MARACAS

Finally, desperately angry, the unpleasant mother grabbed her broom and chased her unpleasant older daughter out of the house. TAMBOURINE

RATCHET "And never return!" RATCHET

AFUCHÊ, MARACAS

And so far as we know the unpleasant older daughter is still traveling the world over, spilling from her mouth whenever she opens it slimy, slooshy toads and snakes. AFUCHÊ, MARACAS

CODA

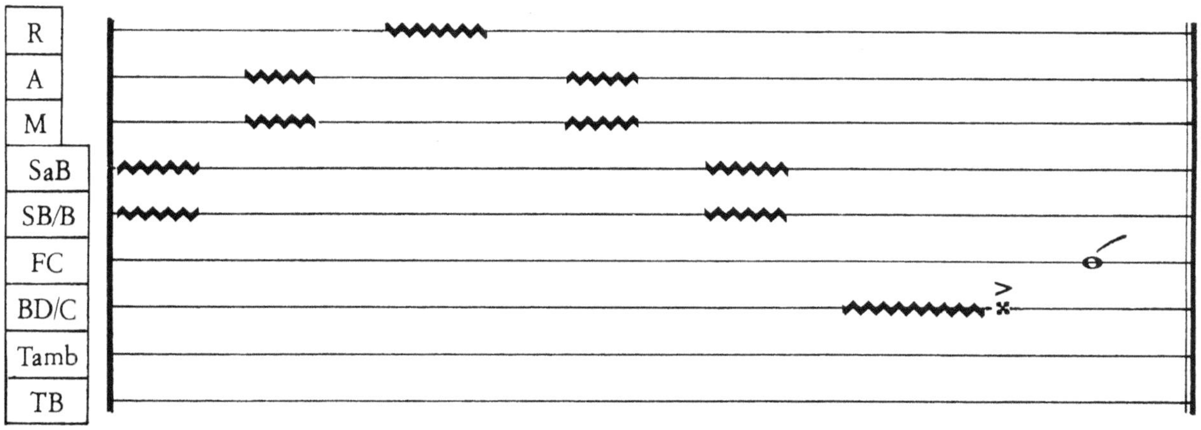

PART 3

Speaking and singing still remain the most important activities. The tonal material of the melodies is increased to seven tones. The children accompany themselves using games and dance forms, with sound gestures, small percussion instruments and eventually, barred instruments. The very few examples of songs in foreign languages should be sung in the original. The reason for this is to evoke an understanding in the child for the sound of a different language and through that an understanding for the people who speak it.

Instrumental playing cannot be practiced systematically within this age-group. The children can, however, be motivated with individual tasks at the instruments from time to time. (The next time it will be someone else's turn!) All children participate in the preparatory exercises. Those children whose parents have acquired a glockenspiel or xylophone for the home will find it possible to develop their playing ability without so much attention from the teacher. To develop good instrumental technique on the barred instruments, the teacher works from the very beginning using both hands as accurately and directly as possible. The bars are struck in a bouncing way without any tension in the posture.

Reading and writing music develops in the two areas of 1) graphic notation and 2) conventional notation. The first is simply an indefinite inspiration for individual or group forms and the second, with its rules and regulations, binds one to the exact repetition of what is written. All models published here can be reproduced on a board or on large sheets of paper or with an overhead projector. It is important that the examples inspire the children to design their own "musical pictures". These designs should actually be tried out and discussed.

Movement includes specific activities in which there is a systematic development of motor skills. These activities are in the areas of spatial awareness, body co-ordination—alone and with a partner, and in developing skills such as balancing oneself or an object, etc. Stories may provide ideas and inspiration for moving. At first the children use their imagination to improvise freely. Perhaps one such improvisation may be chosen and then practiced for improvement. Such movement activities are just as important as the learning of traditional dance forms.

79. Listen to the Drums

☐ to increase the children's skill in rhythmic imitation and to facilitate their ability for playing hand drums

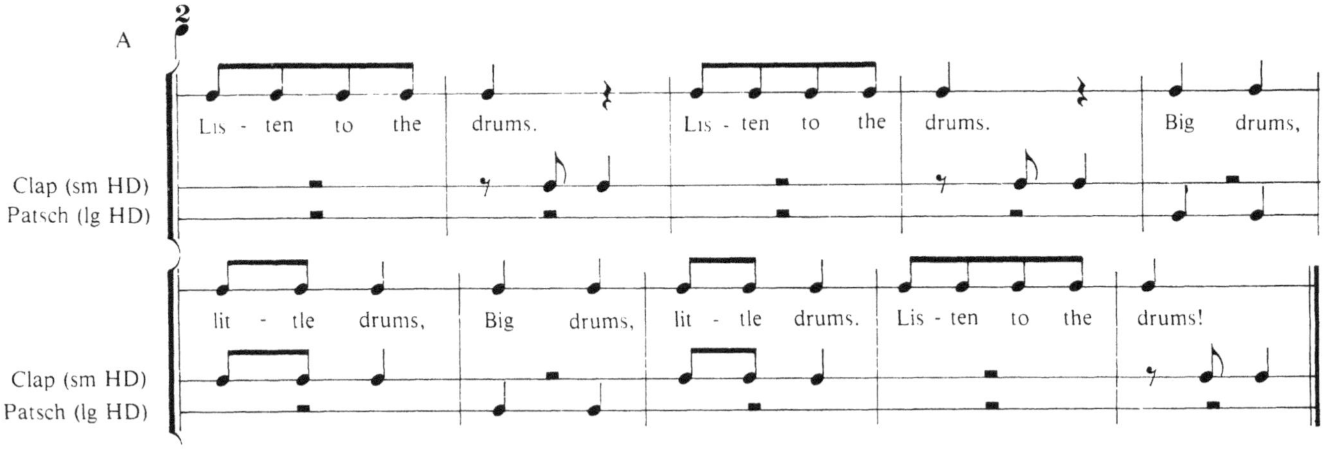

Improvised rhythms; teacher to children, child to child

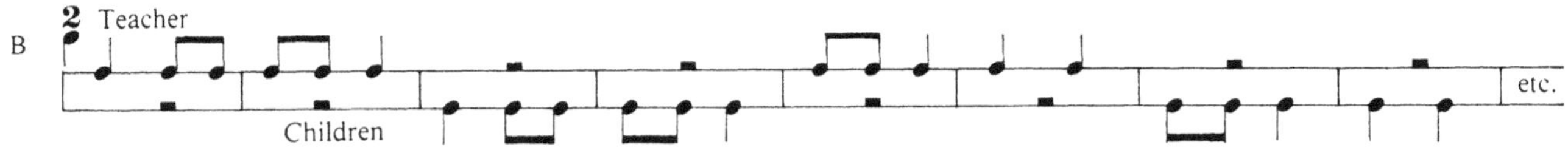

1. Form two lines facing each other. Large hand drums on one side, smaller ones on the other.
2. Teach language with sound gestures.
3. Replace sound gestures with indicated drums.
4. Add part B using varied rhythmic patterns for imitation. Repeat part A.
5. Once words and sequence are memorized by children, "speak" words on a wood block making this a composition for percussion only.
6. Extend part B to practice question/answer rhythms.

From Melody, Movement and Language, *R. and E. Associates, Publishers. Used by permission.*

80. Selected Poetry

Teacher may choose poems suited for the following:

☐ to be accompanied by sound gestures, and/or

☐ to be used for melodic composition, and/or

☐ to create mime, movement, word and sound "pictures"

Linnery, Lannery, Lill

Linnery, lannery, lill.
The ant needs help on his hill.
The fly is too busy, the flea is too dizzy.
Linnery, lannery, lill.

Linnery, lannery, lock.
The shoe walks along with the sock.
The pants and the shirt ran away with the skirt.
Linnery, lannery, lock.

Nonsense Rhymes

I baked a clap of thunder,
I fried a gentle breeze.
When I stirred them all together,
it always made me sneeze.

I climbed a tree of gumdrops,
I swam in lemonade,
I jumped into an ice cream cone—
what a crumbly mess it made!

I washed my face with powder,
I combed my hair with glue,
I brushed my teeth with marmalade,
and now they've all turned blue!

Shoes

Blue shoes, red shoes,
black shoes and brown,
big floppy, sloppy shoes
on a funny clown.

Mousey Brown

A mouse ran up a candlestick,
a silly mousey brown,
to nibble at the tallow and
to act the fool and clown.
He called to friends and relatives,
but they had gone to town;
So he curled up tight into a ball
and "roller-coasted" down.

How do you do, my Old Lady?

How do you do, my old lady?
How do you do today?
I've a pain in my toe, so I know it will snow;
I don't do very well today.

How do you walk, my old lady?
How do you walk today?
I've a crick in my back, for I stepped on a tack;
I don't walk very well today.

How do you sing, my old lady?
How do you sing today?
I've a boil on my tongue, and my fiddle's unstrung;
I don't sing very well today.

How do you eat, my old lady?
How do you eat today?
I've readied a dish of ice cream and fish;
I don't eat very well today.

How do you read, my old lady?
How do you read today?
I've a sty on my eye, 'tis the reason why
I don't read very well today.

What do you well, my old lady?
What do you well today?
I take off my shoes, and snooze when I choose;
That's what I do well today.

Leafy Magic

They're coming down in showers,
the leaves of gold and red.
They're cov'ring the little flowers
and tucking them in bed.
They spread a magic carpet
all up and down the street,
and when we walk along to school
they rustle 'neath our feet.

81. Jingle at the Window

Texas

Children enjoy doing this movement with jingle bells on their wrists.

The Dance

Formation: two lines of six to eight children facing each other.

Verse: The children at the head of the line weave in and out the "windows" and remain at the foot of the line when they finish.

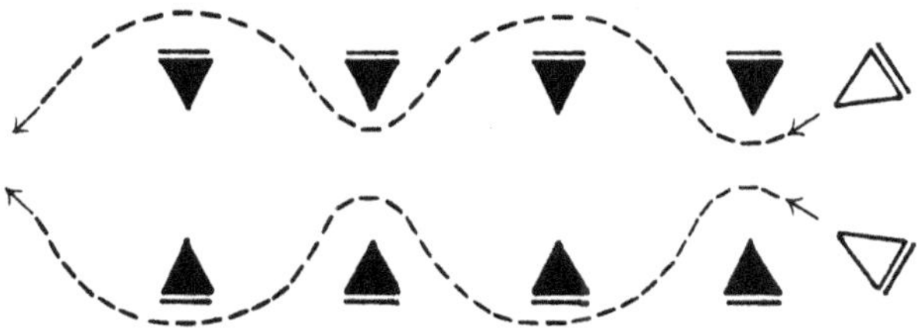

Chorus: Measures 1-2

The traditional bleking or "la raspa" step, done in place:

– hop on left foot with right heel extended

– hop on right foot with left heel extended

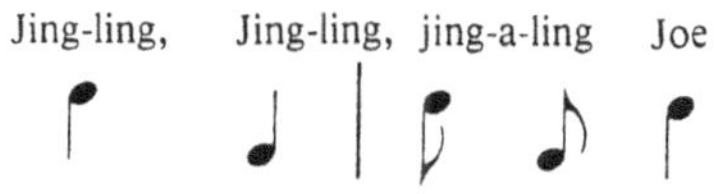

Measures 3-4

The children may enjoy clapping "tideo" each time it occurs in the song with jingle bells on their wrists.

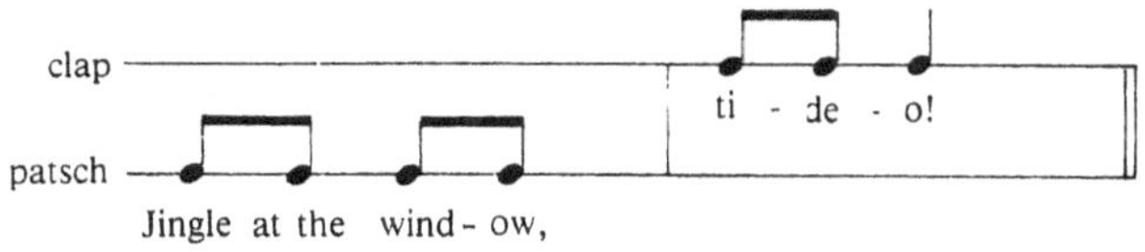

82. Pretty Little Baby

83. Juan Pirulero

Game

All children sit or stand in a circle. One child is Juan Pirulero and stands or sits in the middle of the circle. He makes an extension of his nose with his hands thus: the left hand thumb on the nose and the right hand connects to the left small finger with the thumb.

1st variation: All children pantomime the same thing (usually some type of housework); when Juan Pirulero imitates their actions, the children switch to his nose thumbing.

2nd variation: Every child pantomimes something different; when Juan Pirulero begins to imitate one child, that child takes his action. The others continue their original pantomime. They can also pantomime playing instruments.

3rd variation: Children play instruments. Juan Pirulero does not. When he imitates a certain child that child stops playing his instrument for as long as he imitates. When he stops imitating, the child plays again.

Pronunciation guide: ju = as the word "who"
que = ke as in the word "kettle"
c (as in cada) = k as in the word "kite"

The text means: "This is the game of Juan Pirulero in which everyone must pay attention to what is going to happen next."

84. It Rained a Mist

Possible preparation for AX part:

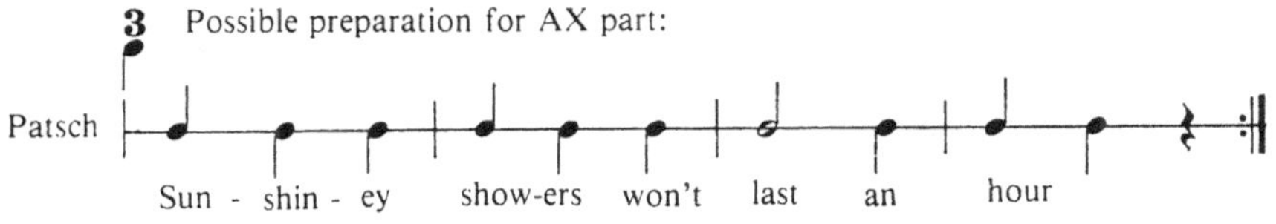

Possible preparation for BX/BM part:

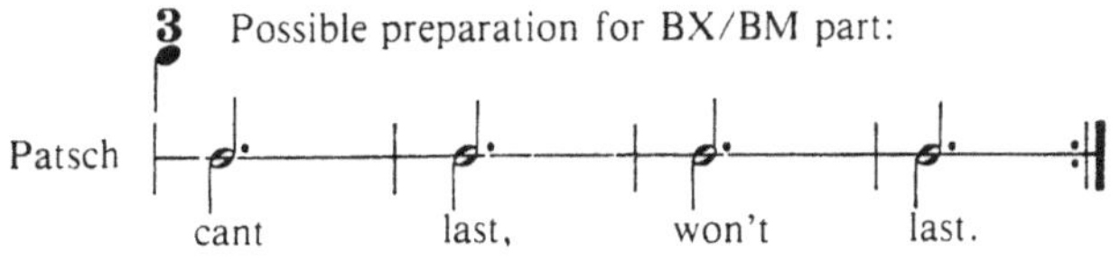

85. Christmas is Coming

1. Learn the verse.
2. Speak the verse accompanied by sound gestures suggested by the children to keep the pulse, or by a silent gesture. Well co-ordinated children may be able to clap or patsch the rhythm of the verse.
3. One child walks around as the "old man", "collecting" from the others with an old hat.
4. The children should have a chance to improvise a melody to this verse.

86. Music Pictures—2

- ☐ to encourage improvisation of simple forms
- ☐ to increase awareness of high and low pitch
- ☐ to further eye-ear co-ordination

The teacher draws large, abstract curves, lines or dots on the board with chalk, and the children try to follow the designs with their voices as they are drawn. Example:

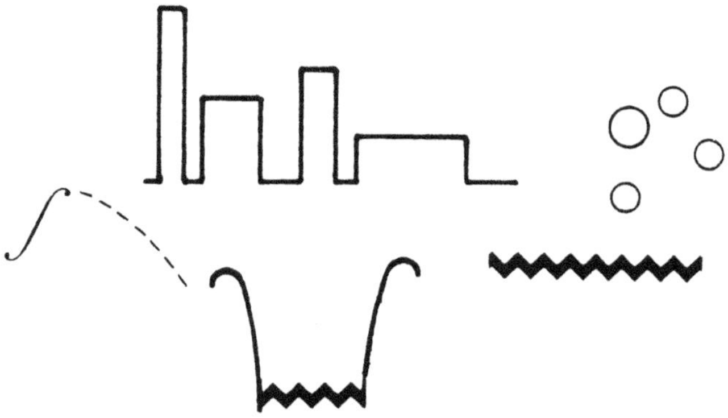

Progression and/or variations:

1. Use colors of chalk, and differently sized pieces on their sides to indicate different timbres, or dynamics. Establish at the beginning what shall represent what.
2. When many designs are on the board, the children can "draw them in the air" as they make the sounds, perhaps in a new order.
3. Let anyone who chooses to do so conduct a "composition", perhaps six or eight designs, following them (as if drawing) with a pointer or handle or a mallet. Encourage improvisation with tempo.
4. On large pieces of paper, the children can draw some of these for each other. Experiment with a pleasing order by pinning or taping some of the designs where all can see them, and move them around as the children choose a plan, or a rondo.
5. This can be extended to movement by having the "composition" transferred to whole-body designs by some children, who can either be accompanied by the rest, or by their own sounds.
6. Another day have the designs "played" on percussion instruments like a new score, perhaps recording or notating it for the future.

87. Short Pieces

These pieces are only models to be used to stimulate the teacher and the students to create their own pieces with notation as an aid to memory and performance.

Some suggestions:

- Use a board, large sheets of paper or an overhead projector.
- Different colors often make some signs clearer.
- Mouth sounds are best represented by their letters or syllables.
- Perform the piece first and make the notation afterwards, or vice versa.
- Teacher works with the children to discover the best sign for the sound intended. (Teacher may want the sound of patsching but a child insists on the vocal, "blup". It is unnecessary to have further discussion!)

Mouth sounds

1

2

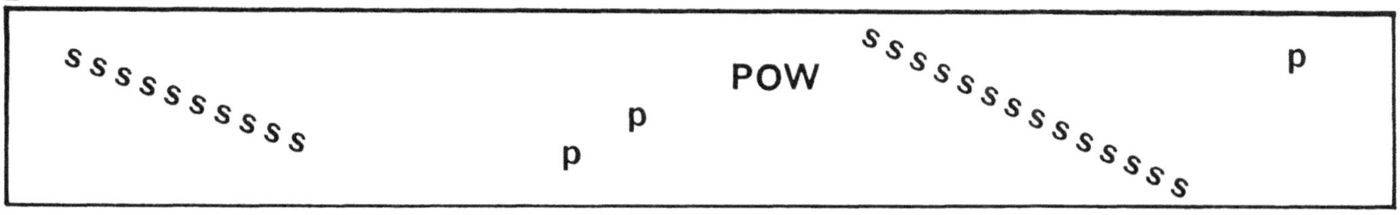

3

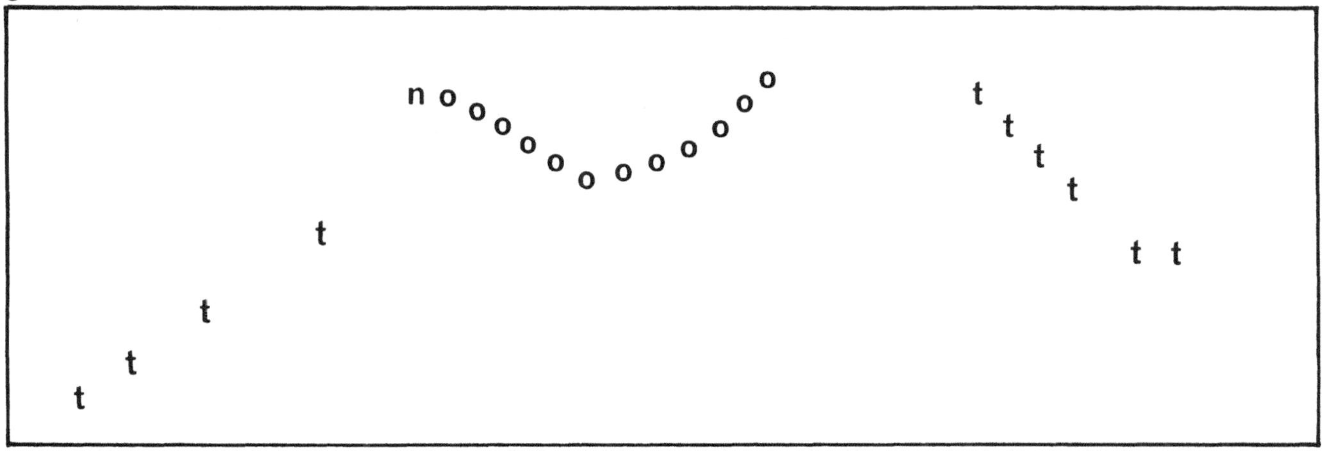

4

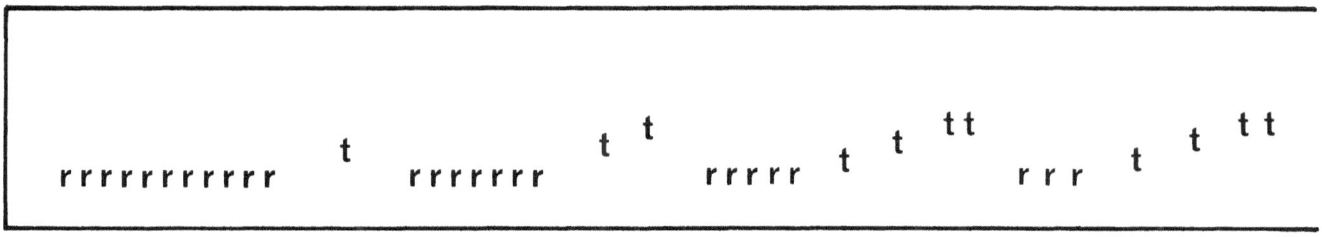

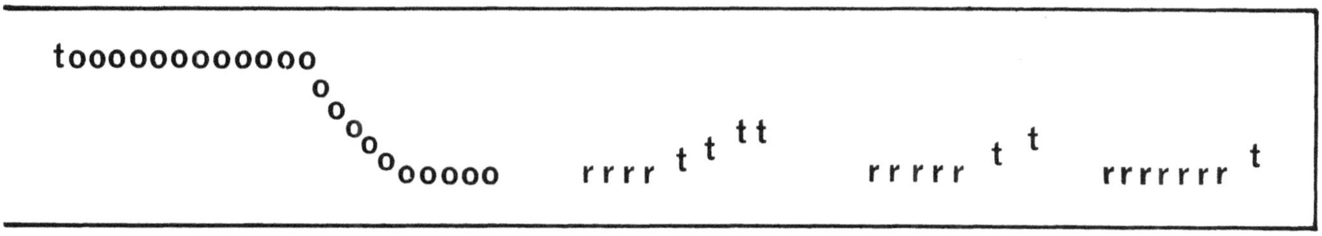

Mouth sounds and sound gestures

Key: ⊥ stamp; = clap; ⊃ cupped clap; ∧ blup!; o lip sound

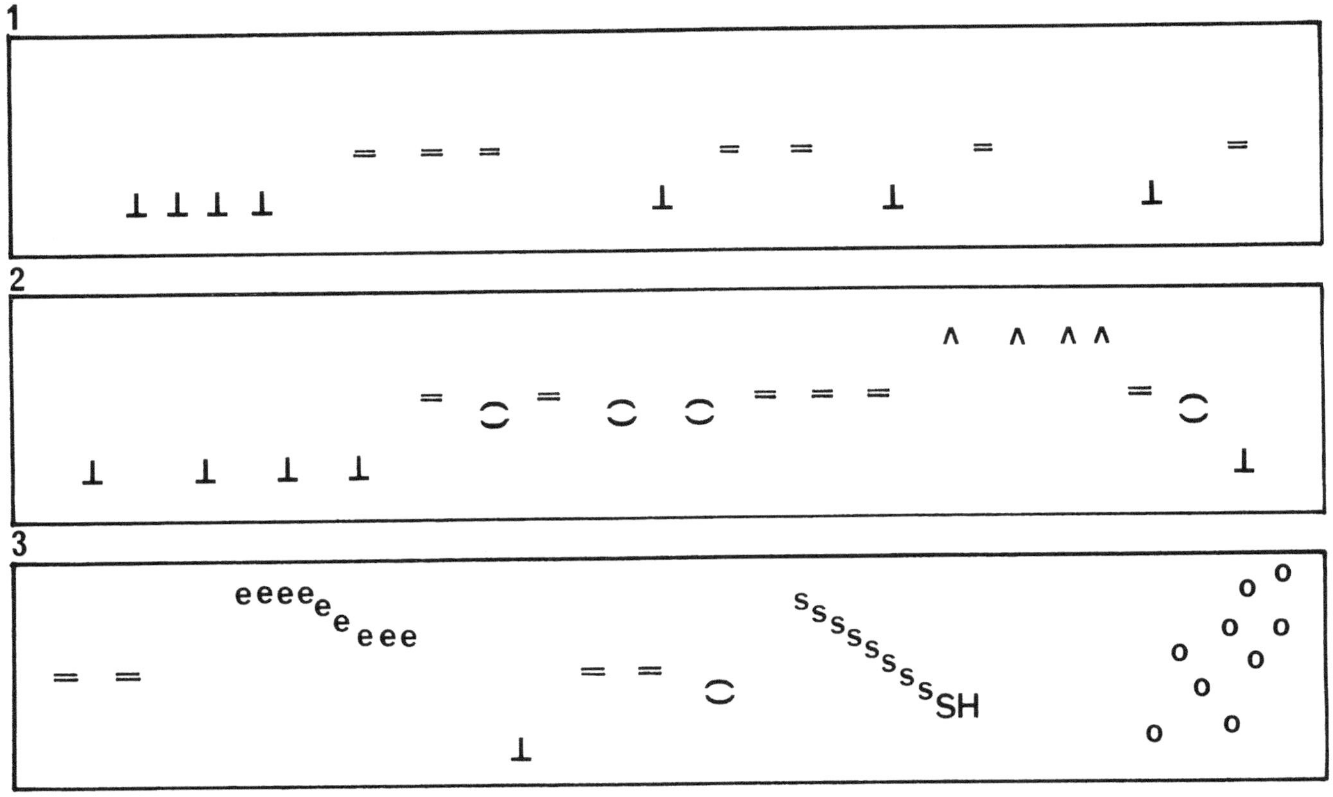

Non-pitched percussion and mouth sound

Key:
• = claves
〰 = guiro
● = hand drum
△ = triangle

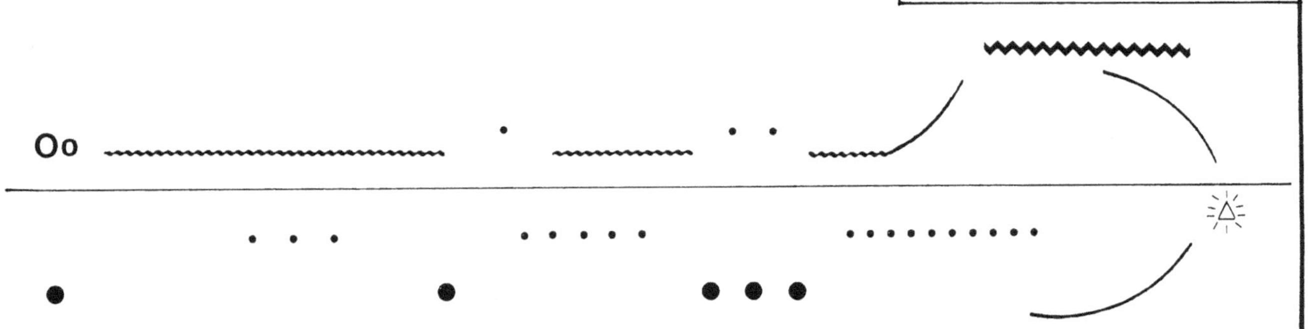

Pitched and non-pitched percussion and mouth sound

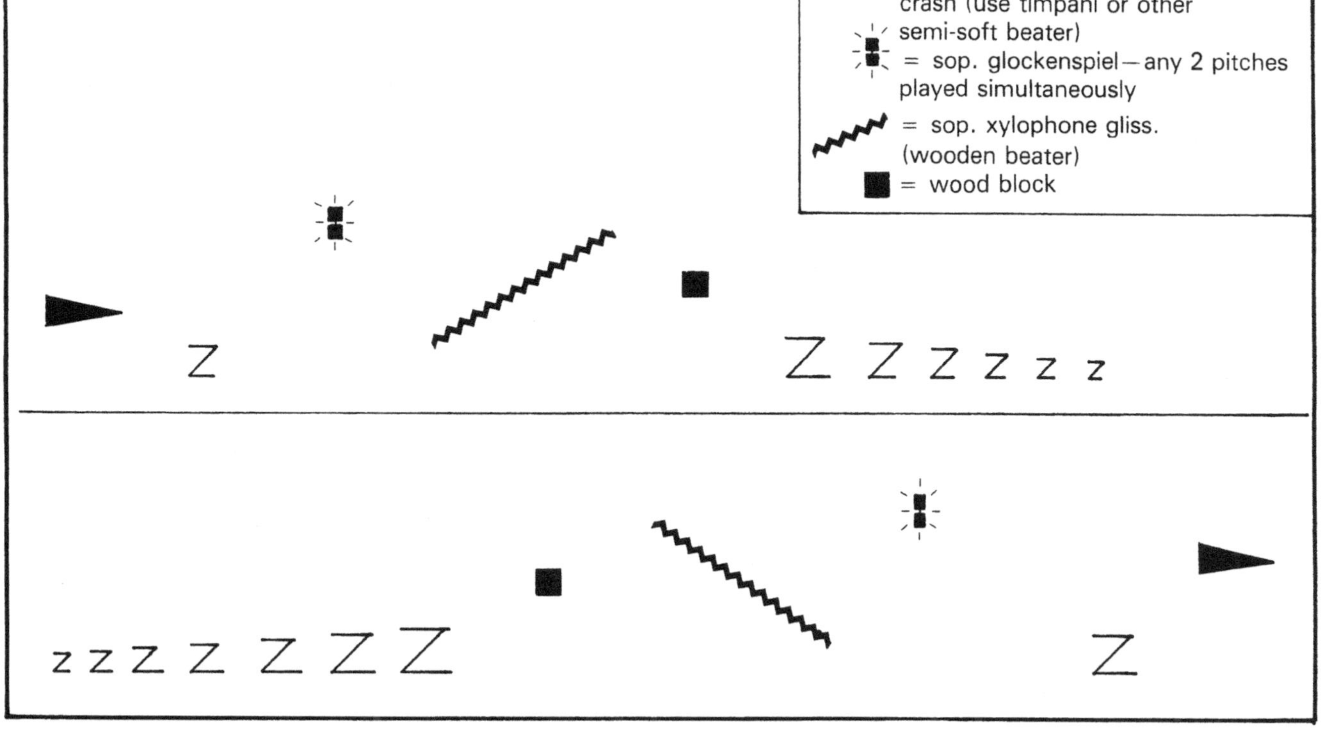

Tambourine and mouth sound

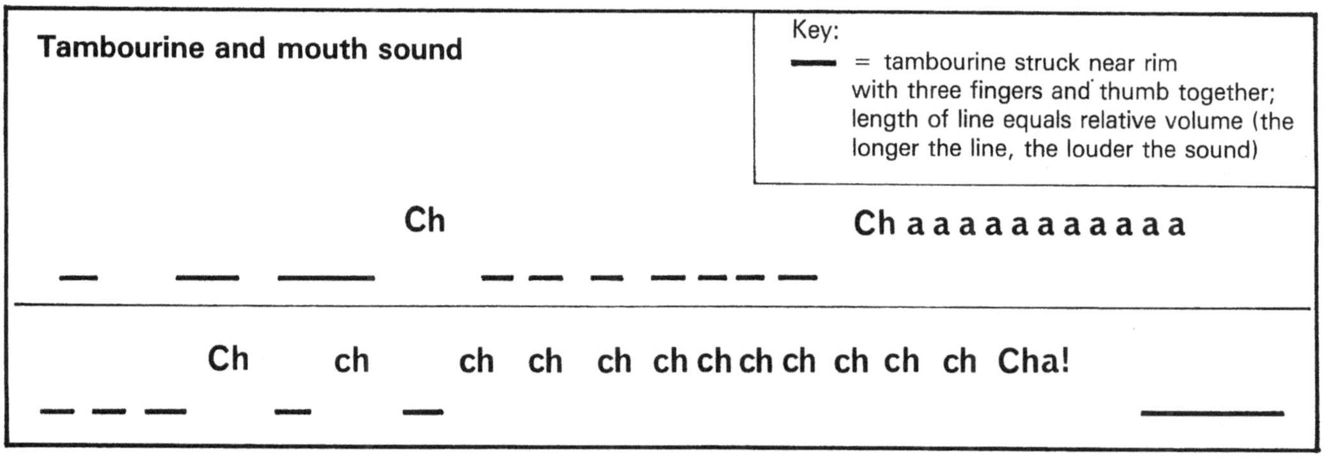

88. Run, children, run

1. While children patsch an eighth note pattern, they echo language phrases of song.
2. Continue sound gesture accompaniment and ask children to echo melodic motifs.
3. Sing Part A and incorporate clap.
4. Teach Part B by echoing language phrases. Change eighth note sound gesture accompaniment to an alternating patsch and clap.
5. Sing Part A with teacher's accompaniment on bass xylophone. The children's accompaniment which has already been prepared through the body percussion may also be added.
6. In preparation for game, children may suggest other ways to move, i.e. walk, hop, etc.

Game: Form a circle with one child chosen as "the sun" on the outside.

Part A: Circle moves left following chosen movement, while the child who is "it" moves in the opposite direction.

Part B: The child on the outside tags someone to chase him and try to catch him before he can move around the circle back to the empty place. If he makes it back safely without getting caught, the child who was tagged becomes the new "sun". If he is caught, he must try again after the song is sung once more.

Possible patterns

89. See-Saw

Two children face each other about 2 meters apart, and pretend to be on a see-saw, i.e. one rises slowly from a crouch while the other begins standing, and slowly squats down. Each child accompanies his movement with vocal sounds, or each may have a kazoo or slide whistle.

Some may discover a matching pitch with their partner, at which time they must hold the tone and a level position in space, like a perfectly balanced see-saw.

Another time, explore other pieces of playground equipment in sound and movement: a sliding board, with slow staccato sounds for climbing the steps and a fast descending "Whoosh" coming down the slide.

90. From Caterpillars to Butterflies

Make a movement story out of the way a caterpillar becomes a butterfly (perhaps after a picture book or visit to a natural history museum).

Later, small percussion instruments can be chosen to represent the caterpillar's life: eating leaves, spinning the cocoon, absolute stillness to mark the passage of time. This can be "illuminated" with a wood block clock, free rubato recorder improvisations by the teacher, some children as wind, leaves, winter snow, and spring rain. Let the children choose and experiment.

Finally, the intermittent pushing, stretching and slow rising to break out of the cocoon. Then the reaching and opening of the wings to dry and the first tentative, circling and gradually expanded soaring flight.

After some experiments and observations of how butterflies move (i.e. flying, darting, stopping, with wings in a very slow flap, soaring and circling, resting perfectly still), small percussion instruments are explored to initiate the movement.

Example

Finger cymbal with striker = fast repeated beats for fluttering
Triangle 𝅗𝅥 𝅗𝅥 = soaring and/or circling
Hanging cymbal = stopping, resting on a flower, slow flap

As long as the sound of the hanging cymbal is audible, the children remain in place, perhaps with eyes closed to sharpen perception. When the sound has faded completely, the butterflies move again, accompanied by the finger cymbal.

These activities may be simplified at first to include only two contrasting movements; stop and go or fast and slow. Later they can be accompanied or initiated by children playing glockenspiels and metallophones, suiting their free improvisation (glissandi, etc) to the movement just experienced.

91. This Old Man

- ☐ to increase the children's awareness of spatial relationships
- ☐ to reinforce a feeling for pulse by playing the instruments
- ☐ to learn the names of the small percussion instruments

A variety of small percussion instruments is spread evenly over the floor area. As they sing the first four measures of the song, the children skip or walk carefully among them, stopping to name the instrument at their feet on the proper beat. During the chorus ("knick-knack") they play that instrument, trying to stay on the beat. At the word "home" the instrument is carefully replaced to start again.

In the beginning, it may be easier to sing the whole song once, moving, and play it once until the children have good control.

If possible, try to have one instrument per child which may include such things as a set of keys, box of beans, bamboo sticks, etc.

> This old man, he played one,
> he played knick-knack on my........(name of instrument)
> with a knick-knack, paddy-whack, give a dog a bone, } (play)
> this old man came rolling home. }

92. Chipewa Lullaby

Suggestions

1. When introducing melody, have children *echo* phrases, entering on the up-beat where teacher is sustaining tied note.
2. Replace or add to the *echo* the melody of AG on glockenspiel and/or recorder.

From Dance Down the Rain, Sing up the Corn, *R. and E. Publishing Company, San Francisco, Ca. used by permission.*

93. Going Right Home

Eric D. Johnson

I left my town to travel,
I left my state to roam,
I left my land to wander but
I'm going right home.

I left my cat some catnip,
I left my dog a bone,
I left my goat a tin can but
I'm going right home.

I left my hat in Paris,
I left my coat in Rome,
I left my shoes in London but
I'm going right home.

I left my friends a-waving,
I left my job alone,
I left my family waiting and
I'm going right home.

This is a verse to march to. When speaking the word "left", step on the left foot, "right", the right foot. Find some floor patterns for a "Grand March" (in single file, with couples, etc. – see examples below – walking or skipping.

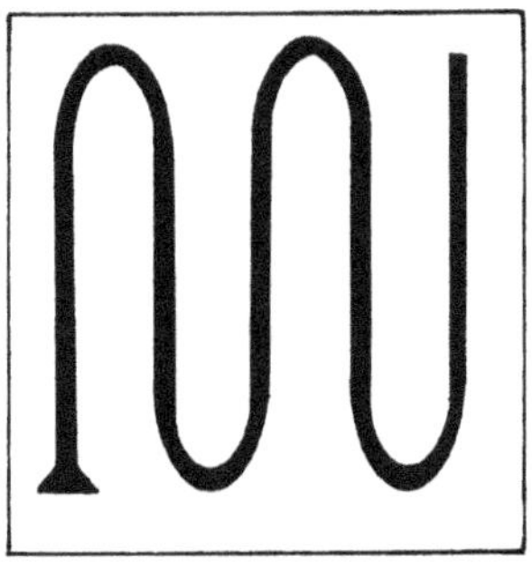

94. His Majesty's Cat

Formation: Children in a circle, sitting or standing.

Teacher says:
"His Majesty's Cat is a *big* cat."
The children echo the sentence.

The next child then repeats the sentence, putting in a new word to describe His Majesty's Cat. For example, "His Majesty's Cat is a *fat* cat."
The group echoes the new sentence. The game goes all around the circle until everyone has a turn to describe His Majesty's Cat.

Variation 1: Ask the children to show a movement that goes with their descriptive word. For example, if the child says "fat", he must also show the word with some kind of descriptive movement. The group then echos the words *and* the movement.

Variation 2: Play the game at Hallowe'en substituting the words:
"A Hallowe'en Cat is a ________ cat."

Variation 3: Establish an ostinato: for example – clap / patsch 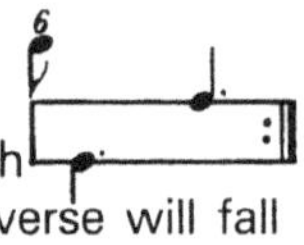
When the ostinato is played, the verse will fall naturally into its own rhythmic pattern.

Variation 4: After the children have given a word, ask them to choose an unpitched percussion sound to be played as they speak their word (or instead of the word).

Variation 5: Add a form to the game by using an introduction (cats meowing and scratching sounds), the game in the middle with the percussion or not, and a coda to end it.

95. Yay Hoo

American Indian Dance

Repeat as often as desired

Accompaniment: Tom-tom plays unaccented pulse continuously.
Dancers wear bells around their ankles.
Boy dancers carry shakers.
Girl dancers carry evergreen boughs.

Characteristic Dance Step: ‖: ♩ Step on right foot, bounce slightly on ball of foot
♩ Step on left foot, bounce slightly :‖

96. Hop Old Squirrel

1. Speak and patsch the words "hop old squirrel", emphasizing the rest with a hand gesture.
2. Speak and clap "deedle dum, deedle dum," and "deedle dum dee."
3. Teach complete language phrases using sound gestures.
4. Teach melody by rote, keeping sound gestures as preparation for instrumental parts.
5. Ask children to suggest other possible movements for the squirrel.
6. Add instrumental parts. Teacher can also add an improvised "B" section on recorder in which the children can move in various ways.

Optional singing game sequence: An inner and outer circle of partners facing each other. Three hops on the words "hop old squirrel," followed by a pat-a-cake sequence with partner on "deedle dum, deedle dum." Do other movements such as, climb, run, etc. as optional second and third ways.

In this case the B section may be omitted.

97. A Paris

From: Gunild Keetman: Chansons Enfantines, *Edition Schott 4890*
B. Schott's Söhne mainz 1958 — p.4

- Children learn to sing the song in the original language by imitation.
- The instrumental setting is too difficult for pre-school children. It can be performed by older children with some instrumental experience. Otherwise it will have to be simplified.
- The words mean:
  1. To Paris, to Paris,
     on a little grey horse.
  2. To Sedan, to Sedan,
     on a little white horse.
  3. We return home
     on a little black horse.
- The song refers to the decisive battle which was fought in 1870 at Sedan, in which the French army lost against the German armies.

98. Old Mother Witch

Instruments may be substituted for the sound gestures as follows:

snap = finger cymbals
clap = guiro
patsch = hand drum
stamp = bass drum

While sitting on the floor, the children can imitate the rhythm of the words by patting their knees, then snapping the first rest, and patting the floor on the second rest.
Explore tempo variations by walking like a limber, lively witch, and then like a wobbling, limping witch. The instrument players must watch the witches carefully to imitate the correct tempo.

99. The Star Game

(invented by the children in Kindergarten, 1975)

- ☐ encourage movement improvisation to quiet music
- ☐ be able to adjust movement to space and length of song

The children lie on their backs on the floor, well spaced over the entire area. Each one figures out a way to "twinkle" (and one will blink very fast!). As they sing the traditional song, one child improvises a dance, moving between them. On the last word, he stops and taps another, and they exchange places to begin again.

If the class is large, two or three stars may dance at once.

Listen to W. A. Mozart, 12 Variations on the French Song "Ah, vous dirai-je Maman", KV 265, for piano solo.

100. The Little Family

Appalachian Spiritual

Note: This song is appropriate for both church choirs and school classrooms. Its traditional classification is a White Spiritual with melodies of English and Irish origin.

101. **Dučec** (Jumping Dance)

A peasant's dance, consisting of various sequences of different jumps which can be combined *ad lib*. Legs and feet are kept quite stiff so that dancers seem like rubber balls, jumping up again as soon as their heels touched the floor.

The musicians play this short melody in different related major keys (occasionally starting on the third above, as if playing a descant to it), the bordun accompaniment follows.

Formation: Either: in a circle, no partners
or: couples dance freely, hands joined or free. Sometimes they take turns in dancing, while the partner just claps and shouts "hey" etc.
Arms: Boys: hands clasped behind back
Girls: hands on hips
Step patterns (to be repeated or combined):

Jump up and Ⓐ ♩ land on both feet, left forward, at one pace's distance
♩ same, right forward
Ⓑ same as before, but with feet crossed
Ⓒ ♪ land on both feet, open position
♪ make heels touch in the air
Ⓓ feet closed, mark ♫ ♩ accents with heels

These patterns can either be repeated over 3 bars or else combined together. All combinations are possible, but ♫ ♩ has to be at the end of each phrase (bar 4).

1. Let children move freely; alone or in twos; like horses pulling a cart or a sleigh; like rubber balls; miming the bouncing of a ball, following it with eyes and hand; with their "ankles tied together"; like "a wooden puppet, made out of one piece"; running, at the end of each phrase (bar 4) clap ♫ ♩ into the hands of another child or, if somebody did not find a partner, on the floor or at a wall.
2. Learn the melody (from different starting notes).
3. Kneel or sit cross-legged: play step patterns with hands on the floor:
4. Children find different combinations and show them.
5. Try same patterns sitting, "playing" with the feet on the floor.
6. Same standing—"experts" can try to turn while dancing their patterns.

Dučec is pronounced "DOO-chets".

(for bar 4)

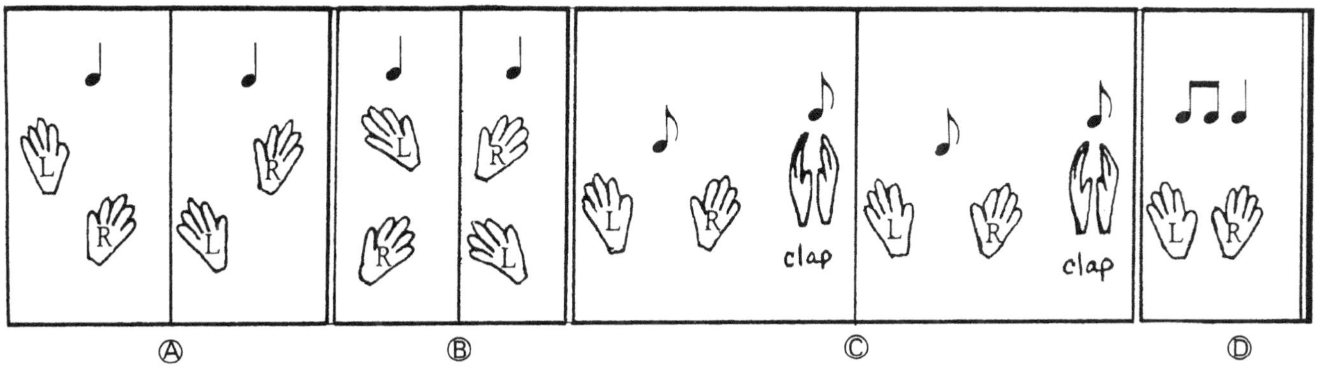

102. **Pussy Willow**

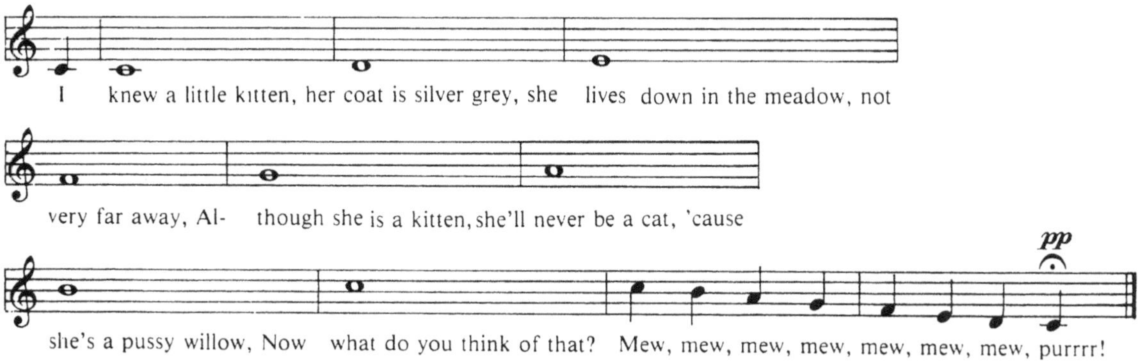

1. After the song is learned well, the children try to show with hands or bodies how the pitch rises in the melody. On the "meow" part, all return to the lowest point by "purrr".

2. Eight children in a row try to sit, kneel, crouch, half stand, etc., to show the relative scale positions of the melody as it is sung. A leader may be chosen to point to the "note person" at his proper place. On "meows", each in turn pops down on to the floor for a repeat.

3. (Notation) If possible, seat the children as above in front of a long piece of scenery paper or a low blackboard. The height of their heads can be marked with a marker, chalk or a sticker in color and transferred to a staff.

4. Many five-year-olds seem to be able to play and hear the steps of this scale quite well. Remove extra bars, leaving an octave; use tone blocks, melody bells or tuned water glasses (a wonderful project for a rainy day!). All sing and play.

5. Scramble the tone blocks or glasses and see who can rearrange them in proper order for the song. Montessori bells work well here.

Using these preparatory exercises as a starting point, it will be easy for a teacher with lots of imagination to continue with traditional notation later on.

103. The End

1. Learn language phrases through imitation with clap accompaniment.
2. Practice clap sequence while speaking words silently.
3. Clapping part may be given to five unpitched percussion instruments, all playing last line together.

from *Now We Are Six* by A. A. Milne (used by permission)

Articles

Movement

Marcia Lunz

From the moment of birth every new movement or motion that a child makes is noted and used in measuring growth and development. The capability to turn over, sit up, creep, crawl, stand and take a step is an important sequence of development. Eye movement, use of hands and response to sounds and words are also analyzed in assessing growth. Since movement is an indicator of life, parenting and educating concerns itself with promoting, encouraging and assisting in its progress.

Children experience delight and satisfaction in the progress that they make. How exciting it is to capture the joy of the child who stands for the first time and marvels in the experience of balancing his/her weight on two feet. There is a persistence in children which enables them to keep trying. They pick themselves up and start over many times in the task of learning to creep and crawl and walk. The desire to explore is a source of motivation as well as the desire to be independent.

Early childhood education assists in the development of the child's natural ability to move and expands the criteria for evaluating growth. Within the framework of imaginative play and creative activities the acquisition of specific skills is stressed. Some of these skills are:

1) Identification and isolated movement of body parts—
   Copy-cat games help to expand the child's experience in isolated movement of body parts. Simple directives to move one foot, raise a leg, put hands over head, etc, will also focus on isolated movement of body parts in addition to demonstrating knowledge of the body part asked for in the directions. Asking for various combinations of body parts to touch the floor will increase concentration and co-ordination; e.g. touch three parts to the floor, or more specifically, have two feet and one hand touch the floor.
2) Development of ability to cross over the midline—
   Suggested activities here can be: a) children sitting in a circle formation pass an object around using only one hand to take and pass the object;
   b) with one hand show the flight of an airplane from the right shoulder to the left shoulder;
   c) rolling over like a pencil or a hot dog.
3) Awareness and recognition of left and right—
   It is helpful at first to mark the right or left (but not both) ankle and/or wrist with a ribbon or band for identification. Consistency in marking the same ankle and/or wrist each time is important. The suggestions given above in (1) can be adapted to include right and left directions. Song games such as the "Hokey Pokey" are fun and strengthen the concept.
4) Strengthening the sense of balance—
   Maintaining one's sense of balance requires concentration that encompasses awareness of the whole body, not just the part that is contacting the floor or other object. Therefore activities should develop the ability to center the body weight in a variety of ways. Beginning work might start with slow motion walking. "How long can you take to make one step?" Later walking in place in slow motion will more consciously focus balancing on one foot. Children enjoy pretending to walk on a high wire and this dramatically focuses in on balance.
5) Combining and co-ordinating the simultaneous use of two body parts—

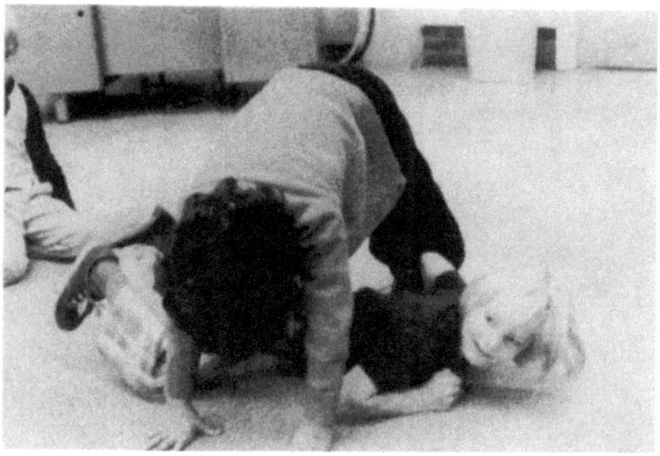

The ability to perform activities of this nature will vary greatly from child to child. Frequent opportunities for combining and co-ordinating movement of body parts will strengthen this skill. A starting point may be the movement connected with a singing game, or walking and clapping to music or a given rhythm.

6) Orientation in space, group and solo—

As the child grows in awareness of his/her environment and other persons he/she begins to build relationships. Young children enjoy the challenge of forming a circle or line or two lines facing each other. Likewise individual children enjoy finding the center of the circle or walking in and out of the circle and other similar tasks.

7) Facility in gross-motor activities—

These activities include walking, running, climbing, crawling, jumping, hopping, sliding sideways, galloping and could well be listed first in the area of skills to be acquired. It is appropriate to state here that sometimes the movements have to be "dissected" in presentation to assist in the performance of a specific task. If, for example, the jump is broken down in sequence, the first part concerns itself with bending the knees and having the arms hanging at the side, ready to swing upward for balance when the feet are pushed off the floor. In a gallop the lead foot leaves the ground while the second foot slides along the floor to catch up with the lead foot.

The child who is experiencing difficulty in acquiring basic movement skills needs to have special attention. Many schools screen children in the area of perceptual motor skills, and those needing remedial work are taken for extra classes.

Props can be used advantageously to initiate and/or extend movement activities for building skills and providing opportunity for creative exploration. An object helps to focus the child's concentration and can enhance the element of play in problem solving. Abstract concepts can be clarified in an experimental way. For example, the meaning of vocabulary words such as under, over, inside, sideways, backward, etc, can be demonstrated with the use of an object. Imagery will also be considered as a prop here because of the direct relationship the ideas have to real objects or experiences in the life of the child.

Simplicity and familiarity are basic criteria for choosing props. Some suggestions are: balls (rubber, foam), hoops, bean bags; remnants of cloth or scarves; balloons, kites; geometric shapes of paper (newspaper, construction paper, cardboard, boxes); rope (jump rope, clothes-line); life-sized, softly stuffed, cloth doll (easy to sew, commercial pattern available); hand puppets, finger puppets and imagery. A few of these props will be considered below with suggestions as to how they might be employed. The list is by no means complete and is meant to be a take-off point.

1) Balls—

Child starts a ball rolling and walks with it or rolls a ball through his/her legs and runs after it. A ball can be kept rolling by pushing it with a foot, elbow, knee, the head, etc. A space can be created with the body like an archway or croquet hoop for a ball to roll through. Arms shaped in an outstretched ring provide a "basketball hoop" and balls can be tossed through gently. Balls can be carried in different ways, e.g. holding the ball between shoulders and head, or between the knees while walking. Partners walking with a ball held back-to-back calls for co-operation. One person has to push and the other has to be pushed, and there is a real challenge in turning a corner!

2) Hoops—

Hoops can be positioned to create a space for crawling between, changed for crawling through, changed again for going under and over.

3) Rope—

A rope can be laid on the floor in a straight or curved line and children can walk alongside the rope,

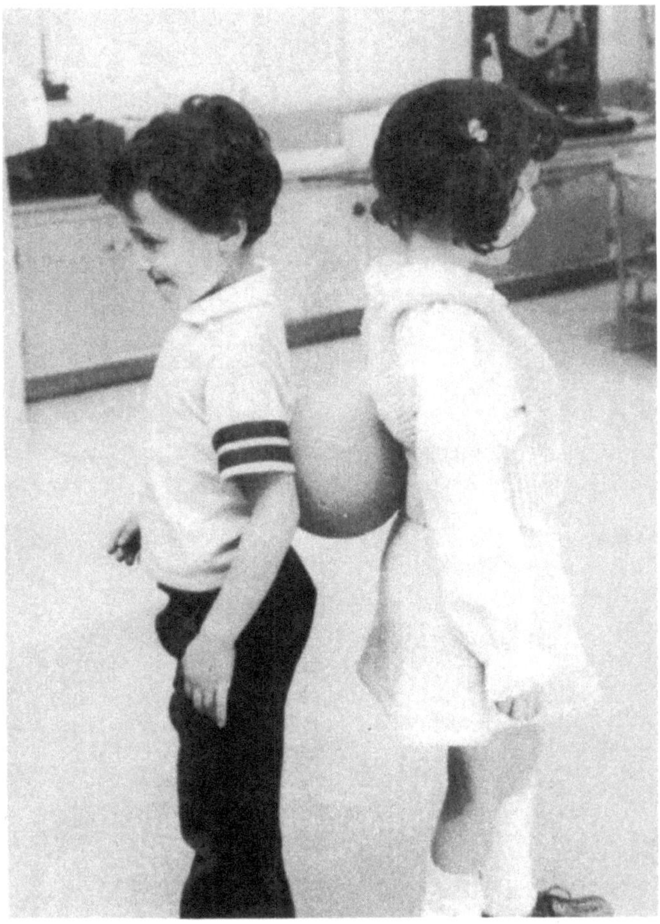

walk sideways facing the rope, or zig-zag back and forth over the rope. Hoops can be used in a similar manner. In the absence of props a tape line, chalk line or painted line can serve the same purpose. The markings on a gym floor provide many possibilities.

4) Cloth doll—

A life-sized, softly stuffed, cloth doll can act as leader or follower for the class. Imitation of the doll's position can build awareness of placement of body parts. The elastic bands on the feet of the doll can be put around the shoes of the child and by holding the doll's hands the child is able to move the doll as he/she moves in space.

5) Imagery—

Children's imagination and innate sense of play-acting should be employed in movement exploration;

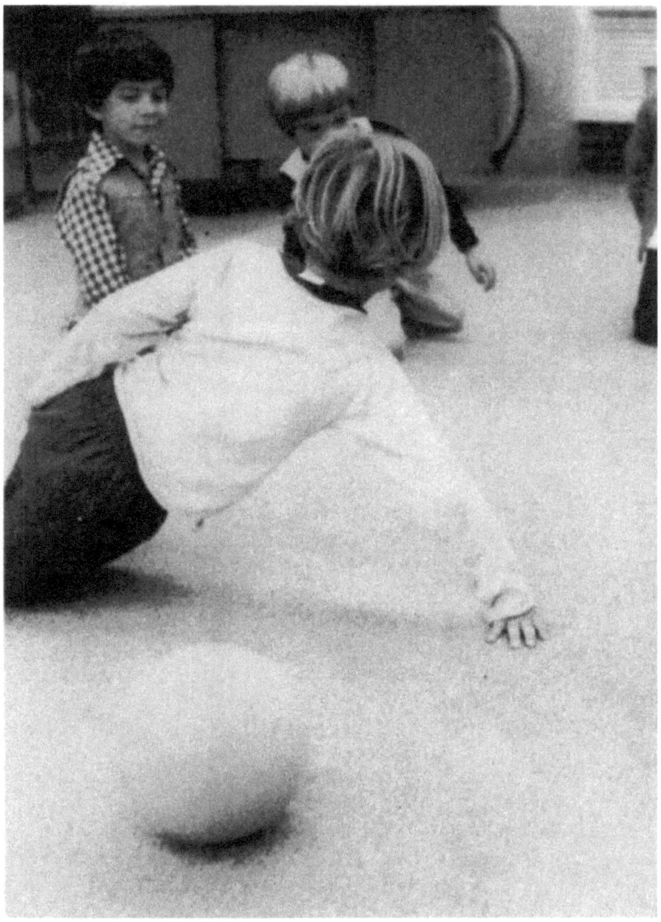

they delight in making themselves as small or as round or as wide or as long as possible and in being challenged to vary the way in which they are doing it. The adjectives that can be applied are numerous. Shapes, such as alphabet letters, numbers or objects familiar to them (donut, snowball, pretzel, etc), intrigue them also, and they are eager to create the shape with their body. The melting snowman, a sizzling piece of bacon in the frying pan, the journey of a three-wheel coaster wagon (fourth wheel is broken) and other similar ideas readily engage the child in creative body movement as well as in an element of dramatics.

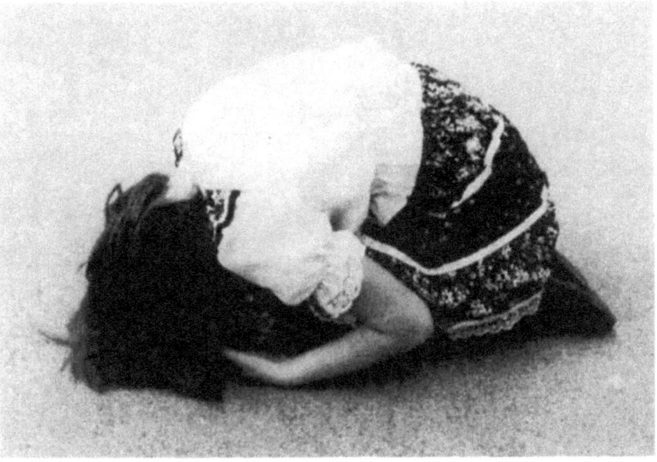

The delineation between play and learning can be a difficult one to make. The achievement of a balance between too much freedom and too much control must be assessed in each situation. All children need to express themselves verbally, physically and emotionally and opportunity for such expression that is creative and constructive will be beneficial. The use of props, as described above, offers one way of focusing the energy, enjoyment and persistence that comes naturally to a child. In every aspect of teaching educators must be aware of the sequential learning that needs to take place in order to build a solid foundation for all future educational experiences the children will encounter.

Play-orientated tasks given to children for skill development are fun, and further movement learning as well as helping to develop skills for dealing with life situations and living in society. The concentration and co-operation experienced in problem solving and creative exploration in the movement class is imperceptably laying a foundation for the future by helping to shape positive attitudinal values and good habits for dealing with tasks at hand.

The Schulwerk approach deals with the child as a whole person; the concepts form a whole. In the educational environment where there is acceptance of children's efforts, positive reinforcement and encouragement to keep learning, the child can grow and develop his/her full potential.

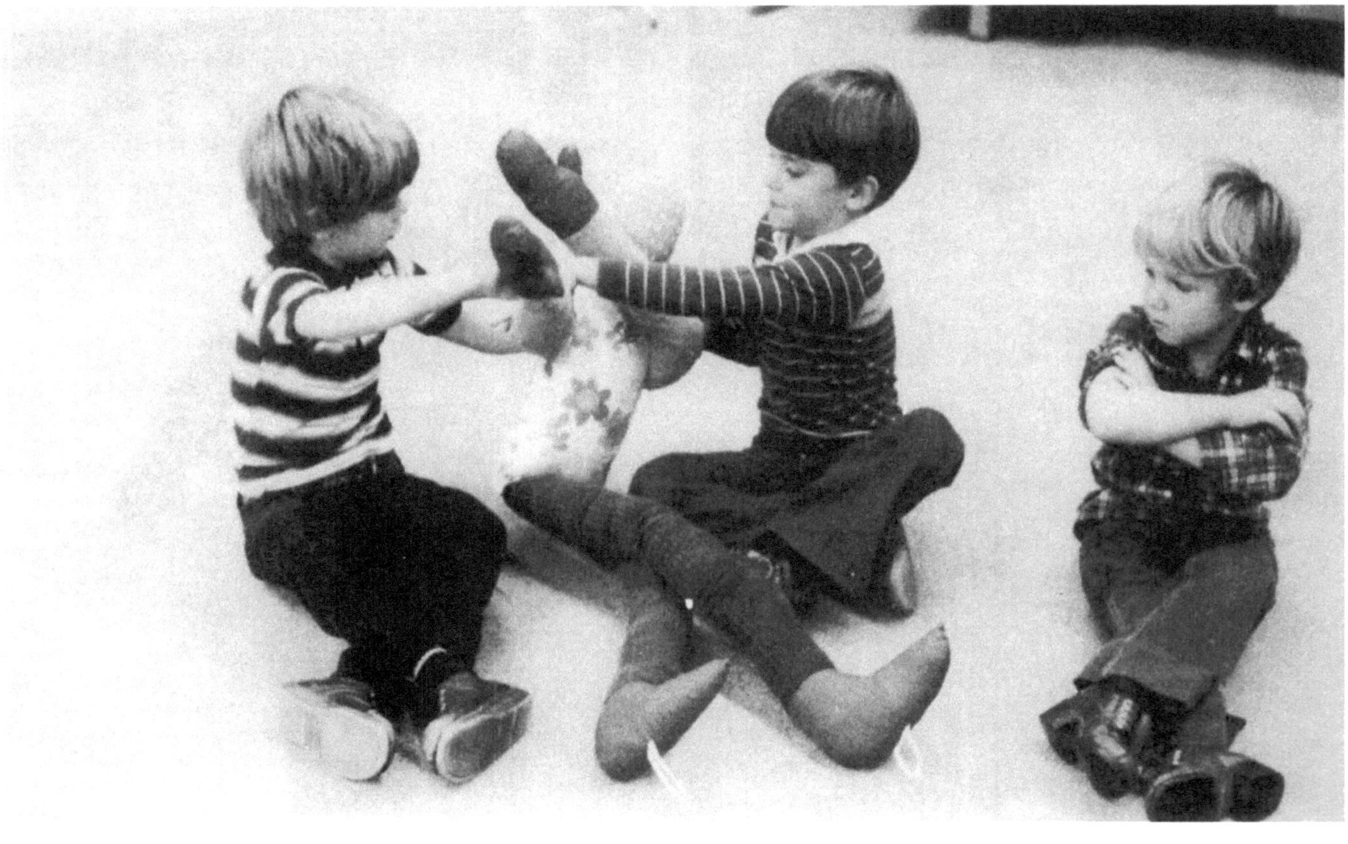

Speech and Song in early childhood music education

Lillian Yaross

The wonder of children learning to speak is one of the most remarkable aspects of human life, since language is the basis of all knowledge and human relationships. Orff-Schulwerk is based on the premise that children can assimilate music in the same way they learn to speak. Both occur because of the child's innate potential for learning and ability to imitate. Speaking and singing, moving and playing every utensil like a percussion instrument, these are both the natural activities of children and the raw materials of the Schulwerk.[1]

Speech development. At about eight weeks of age, children begin to babble sounds, an activity which continues for many months. As they play with sounds, they produce a variety of vowels, consonants, diphthongs, and syllables. Eventually they hear these sounds of their own making. Delighted with their discovery, they imitate their own output over and over again. Imitating their own babbling becomes an activity which provides pleasurable aural sensations as they use a variety of pitches, rhythms, and loudness. Their enjoyment of listening to their own voice inflexions and sounds forms a basis for the next stage: imitation of adult speech.[2]

While in the process of learning to talk, children do not acquire one word at a time before progressing to another. They explore many sensory avenues of expression by utilizing one word to convey several meanings. *Coat* may indicate "let's go out"; the word *ball,* because of its roundness may signify an orange, apple, or balloon. At first, children articulate poorly. Jargon or unintelligible continuous speech often begins around ten months of age and continues for seven or eight months. Gradually as their nervous system matures and memory span develops, children begin to imitate words more accurately, and a refinement process begins. Between fifteen and eighteen months, while energy is concentrated upon walking and other motor skills, progress in talking may be slow. However, at this time, children may listen more intently to what others say. By eighteen months, more words appear along with continued jargon.

At age two, children may have a vocabulary of two or three hundred words, mainly nouns and action words. Other parts of speech, such as adjectives and adverbs, appear later with pronouns like *me* and *my* as children become aware of themselves as a person.[3] The words they learn are in reference to what is heard, seen and experienced. Everything has a name and they love to ask, "What's this?" This type of communication encourages curiosity, thinking, and a sensitive awareness of the environment.

Between the ages of three and five, language grows rapidly if there is an incentive to speak and many opportunities for communication. At this level, children are often enrolled in pre-school and kindergarten programs, where they can explore new play materials and interact with other children and adults, thus providing further language experiences.

Importance of speech activities. Children derive a special pleasure from group participation in rhythmic games based on rhymes and chants. This combination of chant and body action is appealing because of the built-in components of rhythm, imagination, humor and surprise. Memorizing the rhymes is easy and children can engage in almost immediate verbal participation, often combining it with physical or dramatic action. Participation in such activities benefits children's general growth and musical education in several important areas:

Language development. As children hear their own voices join with others, they discern variations in pitch and volume and learn to control and refine these two elements in appropriate ways (elements needed in their singing development as well). Repetition of the games improves speech articulation and increases vocabulary. On an unconscious level, children are experiencing a steady flow of language, phrase and sentence structure: two important factors for language development.

Listening skills. The compelling rythms in chants and rhymes invite concentration on specific words, accents, phrases, and directions. When a crescendo of sound is included with the chant, "One for the money, two for the show, three to get ready and four to go", in addition to a movement that begins with a crouch and ends with a jump on the word *go,* the child is captivated by the teacher's example and immediately "echoes" the chant, dynamics, and movement. Listening pays off in satisfying ways: the ability to start small and to end with a shout and a jump, two things which children love to do. Repetition increases the fun and brings eagerness to hear another rhyme.

Physical co-ordination. Chanting a rhyme with rythmic action requires the co-ordination of many muscles as arms, legs, hands, or fingers move with the chant. When "one potato, two potato, three potato, four, five potato, six potato, seven potato, more" is chanted, one fist is traditionally "hammered" on the other as each number is chanted alternating right and left fists as hammers. Learning to synchronize body language with speech and with other people helps develop the inner rythmic sureness needed for communication and other learning processes such as reading. "Monkey see, monkey do, won't you make up something new?" is a chant that can invite one child or an entire class to "become a new animal or statue" that moves when a tambourine or recorder is played. Because of the play element, children enjoy repeating such games, leading to greater physical control and a developing repetoire of imaginative body movement.

Creative opportunity. Many of the chants and rhymes offer an opportunity for improvisation either with words, actions, or rhythms. Within the structure of a game, children may be asked to think of alternative solutions. As they discover a new body motion, rythmic pattern, or set of words, they are taking the first steps toward creation within a poetic or musical form. Since there are no wrong answers, but rather a wide variety of possibilities within the structure of the game, such contributions by the children enhance their confidence in trying out new ideas in other creative tasks.

The chants and rhymes found in this book come from children's folklore. Some are modern; others date back to the Middle Ages. Single words or objects, counting games, jump rope rhymes, teasing chants, proverbs and poetry are spoken in ways that create intrinsically interesting musical compositions. To these speech patterns, teachers and students become partners in adding something new: a gesture, some movement, dynamic interest, a new and surprising timbre. The words often suggest sound effects which may begin with simple body sounds and lead to accompaniment on various percussion or melody instruments. The aim is to produce a delightful sound and a satisfying musical experience. According to Susanne Langer, "Choric chant, no matter what its poetic content, is essentially music".[4] The chant creates a dynamic form with purely sonorous movement that provides its own audible time experience.

Singing development. In observing two- or three-year-olds at play, we often notice them humming short songs invented while playing. They also try to sing the songs they have heard, often repeating certain words, phrases, or melodic elements, fitting the rhythm to their own movements. In a social setting, the two-year-old does not often play cooperatively with other children, but enjoys when someone plays and sings pat-a-cake, toe- and finger-games with him. Two-year-olds love to play the drum or other instruments, but in their own way. Three-year-old children will often join a group that is singing and dancing, but will sometimes prefer to watch and listen until the material is familiar. Most four- and five-year-olds enjoy the social interaction of the group, singing, dancing, or playing the instruments. Pre-schoolers tend to do one thing at a time: sing, play or move. However, as they mature and the songs become old friends, there is an increasing ability to combine activities.

Young children enjoy a variety of songs, those that invite action, silly or humorous songs, as well as quiet reflective ones. In choosing songs for the youngest children, it is best to select those with few words, but strong melodic and rhythmic repetition. They are the simplest to learn, also the most appealing.[5] Again, they are usually found in our folk tradition and are effective because the melody and words are integrated elements that almost "sing themselves".

In approaching singing from a developmental view, the first songs that are a natural transition from chant utilize the falling minor third (so-mi) as found in many of the traditional favorites of early childhood: "Ring around the Rosie" and "Rain, rain go away". Children build vocal security with this limited range of pitches and a variety of solo singing games can be developed using this familiar motif in a question-answer dialog: "Who has the penny?" "Who's behind the piano?" "Johnny has gone away, where is he hiding?" The child who finds Johnny and sings the answer about Johnny's hiding place can then hide while the rest of the class cover their eyes and sing the chant again. Many informal moments during the school day lend themselves to a spontaneous chant using so-mi-la or other pitches.

As songs with additional pitches are added, technical warm-ups of the voice can be fun too. Ask the children to echo your imitation of train sounds, door-bell sounds, horn honks, animal sounds, or various pitches on nonsense syllables such as "beep-beep-beep". Starting first with a wide vocal range and finally narrowing it down to two pitches, and then one, it is possible to get the class to "tune-up" to the starting pitch of the song about to be sung.

In terms of young children's singing, what kind of expectations should there be? Most important is that children like to sing and do a great deal of singing. They should enjoy the sound of their voices. Keep any body percussion or instrumental accompaniment in the background, never overshadowing their voices. Our own enthusiasm is transmitted as we sing together with children, sharing the joy of many favorite songs. However, in order to clearly hear the children's voices, we must sometimes just listen and enter only when necessary to supply missing tones or words. Children will often sing lustily when we drop out.

We can also expect children to improve vocally by carefully selecting appropriate songs within their range and providing many singing experiences. Children can hear, enjoy and assimilate songs that are beyond their ability to perform well, but their level of accuracy is an individual development process. For the most part, each child selects the song portion that is within his ability to imitate.[6]

Our choice of vocal and instrumental materials can also prepare the way for children's understanding of many musical concepts. If the teacher talks about them in a casual way, the following vocabulary can easily become part of the children's musical consciousness: soft-loud, crescendo, introduction, accompaniment, direction (with hand signals), A and B sections, names of instruments, and the letter-names of notes.

In many ways, singing games are among the most complete musical activities possible for young children. They not only perceive the song through their sense of hearing, but feel it with their own voices and the movement which gives it further expression. There is also a sense of unity between melody and language, and between the musical experience shared by the group. The singing game demands a group, a community. Choosing a partner means reaching out for friendship; following the rules of the game means structure, fun, and perhaps a turn to be "leader". When an instrumental accompaniment is added by the children, another musical dimension is added. This intimate relationship between singing and playing provides a joyful period of music making for both children and teachers.

[1] *Arnold Walter, "The Orff-Schulwerk in American Education", speech delivered at the First Conference, Orff-Schulwerk Association, April 18, 1969, Ball State University, Muncie, Indiana.*

[2] *Louise Binder Scott,* Learning Time with Language Experiences for Young Children *(New York: McGraw-Hill, Inc., 1968), p.2.*

[3] Ibid., *p.9.*

[4] *Susanne K. Langer,* Feeling and Form *(New York: Charles Scribner's Sons, 1953), p.125.*

[5] *Miriam B. Stecher and Hugh McElheny,* Joy and Learning Through Music and Movement Improvisations *(New York: Threshold Division, The MacMillan Company, 1972), p.14.*

[6] *Barbara Andress,* The Little Child and Music, *Multi-Choice Notes, American Orff-Schulwerk Association National Conference, November 14-18, 1979, Phoenix, Arizona.*

Improvisation and the Young Child

Arvida Steen

The young child (two to seven years), through his exploring, action-filled sense of discovery, has a natural tendency to improvise. The small child assimilates new experiences through action, then delights in rediscovery. It is in this constantly enlarging body of experiences that the basis for improvisation is laid. The challenge for the teacher who believes, as Carl Orff suggests, that each child is capable of self-expression or improvisation of music is to provide a myriad of easily assimilated experiences. The second task becomes one of observation, capitalizing on opportunities to see variations in the child's imitative behavior, and to encourage new discoveries in the musical tasks presented.

"What are these simple experiences for the young child?" the reader might ask. The child enjoys movement, and games of action in imitation of the drum, of the teacher's voice, of another instrument, of a simple song, of a short recording, provide excellent sources of sound. Activities which require refined imitation and control follow: echo clapping, echo singing, chanting, transfering word rhythms to sound gestures, then to instrumental sounds are examples. The four basic activities of Orff-Schulwerk—moving, speaking, singing and playing instruments—offer unlimited possibilities for imitative experiences.

The genius of this approach, however, is that the roots of improvisational responses are found in the imitative experiences. As the child imitates the pulse of the drum, then of the song, and later of an example from classical literature, he begins to improvise, to react from his own assimilation of past experiences. An observant teacher can acknowledge and encourage variations of types of behavior in each child. Thus the improvisation experience has begun.

From this example it becomes evident that improvisation can become an integral part of every music lesson from the beginning of the child's education, as it is a part of the way he educates himself. By structuring music activities to encourage the child's natural responses without imposing adult expectations or limits, the freedom to express through movement, speech and song is enhanced. From this informal, imitative-based activity, the teacher can guide the child to more structured improvisation experiences which, through rediscovery and exploration, allow the child to build concepts and skills which lead to maturing musical choices.

The atmosphere in which this process evolves is important. The challenge is to provide clear structures which are natural and uninhibiting to the child. The child, in the early stages of intellectual growth, responds most expressively through movement and non-language sounds. How fortunate for the music director, for music is primarily a non-verbal expression. It is important, then, that invitations to participate come from the music itself, the drum beating, lyrics and mood of a song, the xylophone or recording, augmented only by the shortest spoken directions by the teacher. Directions can then encourage an individual response, in essence an improvisational response, rather than one which is over-directed and identical to that of others. A second ingredient in creating an encouraging atmosphere to improvisation is a well prepared, flexible teacher, who draws from a wealth of material and ideas and is able to adapt quickly when children respond in unexpected and perhaps more interesting ways than anticipated. The third ingredient is the attitude of respect and enjoyment the teacher has for the unique expressive abilities of each child. The teacher is the model for the child's attitude, and together they listen well, respond positively to others, enjoy the unexpected, and are open to the interests of others. Such an atmosphere encourages improvisation.

There are risks accompanying a music program which includes improvisation as an integral part. Long-range goals with flexible means of achieving them are indispensable if the child is to experience meaningful growth. However, improvisation experiences encourage a natural discovery of music and a development of concepts about music which allow the child to have respect for the integrity of his own music as an authentic expression of himself.

Instrumental Work

Maureen Kennedy

At an early age, children should have the experience of playing with all kinds of small percussion instruments. They are best introduced one at a time, in such a way that each child in the group can have an opportunity to use the instrument. The other children should be encouraged to listen carefully to the sounds and to observe those who are playing.

Instruments can be introduced for their own sake, in order that the children become aware of the special timbre of each one and discover different ways of producing sounds on the same instrument. Percussion instruments can also be used to enhance a song in some way: to reinforce a mood or a rhythmic pattern. A gifted child might be able to play a simple bordun on a bar instrument to accompany a song.

The important thing is not to over-use the instrument or to play many of them together simply to keep a beat. The result of this sort of treatment is seldom musical. When in doubt about whether to add an instrument: don't!

It is important for the teacher to play for the children on as many instruments as possible, and for the children to know instruments other than those in the Orff Instrumentarium. This can be facilitated by hanging pictures in the classroom, inviting colleagues, other musicians, parents who can play for the children.

The most important instrument in the realm of music education for young children is the voice. Next in importance are the sound gestures which come from movement activities and which can be used to accompany songs and dances or make rhythmic exercises. It is easy to transfer to small percussion instruments from this point on.

The teacher is well aware of the tremendous energy children have and the difficulty they have in controlling their movements. Instruments are often played rather harshly with little or no distinction of dynamics, tempo and expression. The teacher can help counteract this tendency by presenting activities which demand careful listening and soft, precise playing. There are games which can be introduced to provoke a full volume of sound as a necessary compensation.

In this basic music education, the foundation has to be laid for using the instruments in a sensitive and accurate way.

Listening Experiences for Young Children

Arvida Steen

The appreciation of music is dependent upon sensitive hearing, just as the appreciation of art is dependent upon sensitive sight. One of the basic reasons for listening to music is to foster an inclination towards music and a love for it. Listening should help motivate discovery and exploration, train the ear to be more sensitive, and prepare the ability to make distinctions between different listening experiences. It is important to consider the young person as an entity of emotional, intellectual and senso-motor dimensions.

Young children can listen to music without necessarily having specific listening tasks. The primary aim of listening unconditionally to a carefully selected piece of music is to listen together to the music as a whole.

Some suggestions to consider:

1) The atmosphere for listening should be quiet – a feeling for calmness within the group. Movement, drawing or painting to the music, simultaneous notation and imitation of the instruments, always popular with children, are necessary methodic steps. Their importance, however, decreases as children become more aware of their own powers of observation, emotions, and their ability to make comparisons.

2) The examples should be short. Listening activities should not be placed at the end of a lesson: the children must be physically and mentally alert as well as highly motivated.

3) Listening to live music motivates much more than listening to records or tapes. Opportunities to present live music should be sought often. Listening to recorded music should also be practiced when one considers that throughout life most music comes from the mass media.

In addition to listening to music without a given task, it is also important to draw the attention of the children to specific elements occuring in the music they are hearing. When opportunities are planned carefully, children are able to hear with a high level of discrimination and their enjoyment of music is enhanced.

Two conditions must be present to encourage children's focused listening. First, the children must be given a clearly defined listening task which is directly related to the music. These tasks are most beneficial when they are objective, rather than related to feelings or subjective opinion. Examples might be to listen for a rhythm pattern, ♩ ♩ ♪.♬ ♩ "About Strange Lands and People", *Scenes from Childhood,* Robert Schumann), or a familiar melody ("Pumpkin Eater's Little Fugue", Robert McBride). There are many ways to prepare children for listening tasks. One particularly helpful way is to begin listening while lying on the floor, eyes closed. This assures the individual focus before group tasks are explored. Returning to this position often renews the child's focus, screening out the other distractions in the room.

The second condition which encourages discriminating listening is to hear the music many times. Music becomes more enjoyable with increased familiarity; and quickly changing variety, for young children, may only increase confused inattention. By giving the children a new task with each hearing, they not only remain interested but they hear more in the music, increasing the value of the music's communication. Thus it is important to play a favorite recording requested by the children long after it has been initially introduced and explored.

It is important to remember, as well, that children enjoy and benefit from listening to recordings of their own music. Even young children can be careful evaluators of their own performance. This also relieves total responsibility, and the sometimes negative effect, of evaluation and teacher judgement. Recording, followed by listening, discussion and re-recording again, can give children a realistic and rewarding sense of accomplishment.

Using Rhymes and Poetry with Young Children

Martha Pline

If it is true that "in the beginning, there was rhythm", then rhythmic speech must have been created on the second day. The youngest child responds with delight to the rhythmic play of "Pat-a-cake" and "Ride-a-cock-horse". For children in the pre-school years, rhymes and poetry have an important place in the school day.

Heritage rhymes fall into two categories: those which originated with children and which are passed from older child to younger, and nursery rhymes. The former may be jump-rope chants, counting-out rhymes, or rhymes for occasions such as the end of school. In contrast, nursery rhymes, many of which originally had veiled political connotations, are transmitted from adult to child. Early childhood educators believe that nursery rhymes are "real" poetry, and thus are as important to the child's development as appropriate folk songs, and as valuable to young children as poetry by known writers.

There are many reasons for the high value of nursery rhymes. Since they happen in the realm of fantasy, they are not culturally biased. Their repetitive quality and the variety of rhyme scheme present children with clear models of form, from which formal principles can later be made conscious. The nonsense words help children in their own word play. The teacher can further encourage the children's experimentation with rhyming and alliteration: children enjoy coming up with such sillies as "Wigglety, bigglety, bop". Both form and rhyme are an aid in developing the child's auditory memory. Children seem to respond to nursery rhymes in a deep, instinctive manner. Perhaps these rhymes retain vestigial shreds of magic about them!

Young children often use a rhyme as an unconscious accompaniment to their own activities. One might hear a recently-learned rhyme being chanted boldly by a group of children as they step from one pavement square to another in the playground, being quietly and meditatively spoken by a child engaged in solitary play, or varying as a child changes coloring pattern with his crayon. In such activities lie important clues for teachers as to how rhymes may be used. And because one need not be concerned with doing justice to the intent of the writer, heritage rhymes may be used and "performed" in a variety of ways.

Pulse-keeping is the most obvious activity. Children can clap, patsch, or (more difficult!) walk the beat. They may be asked to improvise their own pulse-keeping movements, or one child might be the leader with others following. The children discover the concept of tempo by finding the pulse in a rhyme spoken at varying speeds.

By the age of five, some children will be able to clap or patsch the rhythm of the words: "Can your hands say the words, so that the rest of us can recognize what you are clapping?" For this purpose, children's own rhymes are more appropriate, since they tend to be in 2/4, in which the eighth notes are more easily performed than in the 6/8 meter of the majority of nursery rhymes.

By varying the manner of performance (to the great delight of the children), the teacher can present most of the important basic musical concepts: high/low, soft/loud, fast/slow, staccato/legato. Initially each should be presented as a widely varying set of contrasts. At first, for instance, a rhyme can be spoken very softly, then very loudly (but *not* yelled). Gradually the idea of crescendo and diminuendo may be introduced. The stage is then set for later introduction of terminology. Such activity need only take a few minutes of the music period, but pays large dividends in conceptual learning.

Rhymes can be used for locomotion, with 6/8 meter especially helpful for skipping and galloping. They may also serve as an impetus for free-movement improvisation, perhaps suggested by words they contain: falling, running, jumping, hopping.

Improvised chanting of rhymes frees the children's voices and promotes expressiveness. The problem of singing in tune is avoided, and solo singing thus becomes more confident. The teacher can encourage individual children to use neglected parts of their vocal registers.

So far we have considered rhymes realistically, and as vehicles for conceptual learning. Let us now look at using the *content* of rhymes and poetry.

Drama immediately comes to mind. The situation given in the poem forms the story framework; dialog (in addition to that already present in the poem) should be improvised by the children, and should proceed at their pace. Such dramatic play should not be forced into any preconceived time frame, and should certainly not take place while the rhyme is being sung or spoken. Miss Muffet and the spider, for instance, may have a long, short, or non-existent conversation, depending on the personalities of the actors; the only datum is that the spider sits down next to Miss Muffet and eventually frightens her away.

Finally, poems and the images of poetry can be used to set a mood for sound or movement improvisation. Such an improvisation might be based on being at the beach, or on the theme of "rain". Children might express how rain sounds, how it feels to be in the rain, or how rain makes them feel. A teacher can choose from many fine poems to help the children start this activity. It is not necessary for the teacher to explain the imagery of the poem; the material need only be of good quality, and have to do with a subject the children know about.

We need to remember that poems are evocative, and we must let them evoke whatever they will in children, regardless of what we teachers might have in mind! I do not believe that performing already given settings of lyric poetry in sound and movement—however lovely they might be, and however valuable for setting standards and giving examples—is appropriate for pre-school children. They do not yet possess the analytical skills to perform the task with understanding. Reading or speaking of the poem should serve as a starting point for the children's *own* expression of the ideas or feeling which the poem may have evoked.

Involving Parents

Virginia McGivern

Many things are necessary for a music program to thrive in a school: among them an enthusiastic teacher, a supportive faculty and staff, a sympathetic school board. In addition, and just as important, there must be support and feed-back from the parents of the students.

Perhaps the only time one might see a parent is at a concert or open-house designed for the parent as "audience". The parent takes a passive role as observer and "approver" or in some cases as "disapprover".

It is obvious that parents cannot spend a lot of time in the school. How then can we elicit their support for our efforts with our students, their children? Here are some suggestions that might help.

1) Familiarize the parents with the contents of the childrens' music classes. Issue an invitation to visit the classrooms during a specific week or to sit in on the child's instrumental lesson. A curious parent will often be able to answer his own questions about his child's musicality while observing class work. This may stimulate an interest in encouraging certain kinds of behavior at home. The parent also has a chance to ask why certain things are taught and how. Sometimes a parent who wishes to become more involved sees that an accompanist is needed for the choir on Tuesdays. Since he plays the piano, he might offer his assistance!

2) Organize an "Awareness Workshop" where the parents come to school to learn what their children are learning. They might find that music has many other avenues than song and instrument and that it is possible to educate an entire person through musical assistance. Their awareness of what is being taught can have a profound effect on the child at home. They might even realize why more glockenspiels are needed!

3) If you need assistance, let it be known! Often the teacher takes too much upon himself when there is a ready, willing and able parent to make the job go a little more smoothly.

4) Make the parent-community aware that things are happening by extensively publicizing such things as concerts, rehearsals, operettas, operas, plays, recitals, etc.

5) Bring other artists to town to perform for the community. It is good for the parents to experience things *with* their children. One might select an instrumental ensemble (classical, folk, rock, baroque, etc) or singers, or a children's group or a play: the important thing is that it be a live performance.

The parent can also become involved in his own home in helping his child's musical growth and education. Here are some suggestions:

1) Provide a place for the child to practice his instrument or sing which is quiet and uncluttered. The child likes to know that there is a special place for him to play when he has the need or desire. Children may be easily distracted so it is preferable to create an uncluttered atmosphere. Most children, when very young, practice rather sporadically. It might be a good idea to schedule a definite time each day for this activity. The time should be convenient for the child who should discuss arranging the time together with the parents.

2) Look for announcements of special events of musical interest (television guide, newspaper, posters, etc), to see what is available and potentially interesting for the child.

3) Play recordings of one's favorite kind of music – Bach to Blue Grass. Expose the children to as many different kinds of music as possible. The world of music could be compared to a museum: one can wander through and listen to the music of the past and hear how people have changed from all corners of the world – as one approaches the present one hears how we live and think.

When the child is more informed about the people from other times and other parts of the world – their thinking, their feelings, their present-day activities – then his mind is better opened to the idea that music is an integral part of all human societies.

Perhaps, since music is all around us, we should be aware of it and encourage it to grow in our lives. By working together – teacher and parents and child – we can find its relevance for living, studying, playing, enjoying.

We thank the publishers concerned for their kind permission to use their materials.

Arrangements and translation of materials
Lucrecia Arroyo
Joyce Auchincloss
Carol Erion
Dorothy Lyons
Verena Maschat
Virginia McGivern
Miriam Samuelson

ORFF SCHULWERK AMERICAN EDITION

Orff-Schulwerk American Edition

Main Volumes	**Music For Children 1**	Pre-School
	Music For Children 2	Primary
	Music For Children 3	Upper Elementary
Supplementary Publications	*Material for Speech, Dance, Vocal and Instrumental Music*	
	Jane Frazee	Ten American Folk Carols
(to be continued)	Hermann Regner	8 Minatures for Recorders and Orff Instruments
	Sue Ellen Page	Four Psalm Settings For Treble Voices and Orff Instruments
	Miriam Samuelson	Kukuriku Hebrew Songs and Dances for Recorders and Orff Instruments
	Donald Slagel	Circus Rondo
	Richard Gill	Have you any Wool? Three Bags Full! 17 Traditional Rhymes for Voices and Orff Instruments
	Carol Erion/ Linda Monssen	Tales to Tell — Tales to Play
	Ruth Hamm	Fence Posts and Other Poems
	Isabel Carley	Recorders Plus I
	Sara Newberry	Quangle - Wangle Hat

Schott New York

INDEX

Page Number	Title Number	Title	Contributor	Sample lesson	Song	Song with foreign text	Speech piece	Developmental text	Rhythmic exercise	Free meter	Improvisational development	Compositional exercise	Game	Movement response	Movement form	Dramatic response	Instrumental activity	Listening activity	Notation skills	Accompaniments: Sound gestures	Accompaniments: Instrumental ostinato	Accompaniments: Instrumental non-ostinato	Number of tones in melody
2	1.	Name Play 1	D. Lyons	•																			
2	2.	Cuckoo	N. Ferguson	•	•								•								•		2
3	3.	Riddle Me	Editorial Example		•			•				•											2
3	4.	Singing Stories	T Aaron	•																			
4	5.	Wee Willie Winkie	Editorial Example		•																	•	3
4	6.	Bounce the Ball to Jericho	N. Ferguson	•	•									•					•		•		3
5	7	The Penny Game	L. Yaross								•		•										3
6	8.	Elevator	T Aaron										•						•				
6	9.	Hot Cross Buns	M. Kennedy		•															•			3
6	10.	Suo-Gan	M. Pline		•																•		3
7	11.	Vihmakene, Vellekene	M. Kennedy			•					•						•						3
7	12.	Leo and Lamb Chop	M. Pline	•													•	•					
8	13.	Little Jack Jingle	Editorial Example		•																	•	3
8	14.	Circle Travel Game	M.Lunz		•								•	•									4
9	15.	Spool and Key	N. Ferguson		•								•								•		4
9	16.	Playtime Chants	V Ebinger					•															
9	17	Several Animals	T Aaron											•			•						
10	18.	Order in the Court	Editorial Example		•															•			4
10	19.	Up and Down	Editorial Example	•										•				•					
11	20.	Johnny works with One Hammer	M. Burnett		•								•				•						4
12	21.	Travelling	T Aaron		•								•										5
12	22.	Name Play 2	V Ebinger					•															
12	23.	Footprints	T Aaron														•		•				
13	24.	Stars Shining	M. Burnett		•								•								•		5
13	25.	High-Low	T Aaron											•				•					
14	26.	In the Evening	M. Kennedy		•																•		4
14	27	The Ball Game	I. Carley	•	•									•									4
15	28.	Postman	T Aaron		•								•										6
15	29.	Scarves	T Aaron	•										•				•					
16	30.	Mary Wore a Red Dress	M. Burnett		•								•										5

INDEX

INDEX

																						Accompaniments			
Page Number	Title Number	Title	Contributor	Sample lesson	Song	Song with foreign text	Speech piece	Developmental text	Rhythmic exercise	Free meter	Improvisational development	Compositional exercise	Game	Movement response	Movement form	Dramatic response	Instrumental activity	Listening activity	Notation skills	Sound gestures	Instrumental ostinato	Instrumental non-ostinato	Number of tones in melody
31	61.	Corn Grinding Song	M. Burnett										●								●		5
32	62.	Candle Suite	A. Steen		●		●	●												●	●		5
32	63.	Old Jeremiah	V Ebinger					●															
33	64.	Jack Be Nimble	T Aaron	●	●								●										4
33	65.	Sound Signs 2	Editorial Example							●							●		●				
34	66.	There Was an Owl	Editorial Example		●																	●	5
34	67	Easter Eggs	T Aaron	●			●							●						●			
35	68.	Lou Pripet	Editorial Example												●						●		6
35	69.	One Misty, Moisty Morning	M. Burnett				●							●			●					●	
36	70.	Hiding Chant	V Ebinger					●					●										
36	71.	Jack and Gill	Editorial Example		●																		6
36	72.	Happiness	M. Burnett				●										●			●			
37	73.	I Like Coffee	A. Steen				●						●	●									
37	74.	Three Wise Men	Editorial Example		●																	●	5
37	75.	Introducing the Hand Drum	M. Pline	●					●								●						
38	76.	Dynamics	M. Pline	●																			
38	77	Sound Signs 3	Editorial Example							●							●		●				
39	78.	Fairies	V Ebinger				●			●							●					●	
44	79.	Listen to the Drums	M. Burnett				●										●			●			
44	80.	Selected Poetry	R. Hamm					●			●	●		●		●							
45	81.	Jingle at the Window	M. Burnett		●										●						●		5
46	82.	Pretty Little Baby	M. Pline		●															●			5
46	83.	Juan Pirulero	Editorial Example			●							●										5
47	84.	It Rained a Mist	A. Steen																		●		6
48	85.	Christmas is Coming	M. Pline				●				●					●							
48	86.	Music Pictures 2	T Aaron	●							●			●				●	●				
49	87	Short Pieces	E. Nielsen									●							●				
52	88.	Run, Children, Run	M. Burnett		●		●						●							●	●		5
53	89.	See-Saw	T Aaron	●										●									
54	90.	From Caterpillars to Butterflies	T Aaron	●							●			●		●	●						

INDEX

ALPHABETICAL INDEX

(by page number)

Orff-Schulwerk American Edition

Main Volumes

Music for Children 1	Pre-School	**SMC 12**
Music for Children 2	Primary (*revised edition*)	**SMC 6**
Music for Children 3	Upper Elementary	**SMC 8**

Supplementary Publications

EIGHT MINIATURES
(Hermann Regner) **SMC 14**
Ensemble pieces for advanced players of recorders and Orff instruments which lead directly from elementary 'Music for Children' to chamber music for recorders.

CROCODILE AND OTHER POEMS
(Ruth Pollock Hamm) **SMC 15**
A collection of verses for use as choral speech within the elementary school. Included are ideas for movement, instrumental accompaniments, and proposals for related art, drama and listening activities.

THE MAGIC FOREST
(Lynn Johnson) **SMC 16**
Sequenced, early childhood, music-lesson plans based on the Orff-Schulwerk approach.

STREET GAMES
(Gloria Fuoco-Lawson) **SMC 17**
Instrumental arrangements of rhythmical hand jives based on traditional American street games.

DOCUM DAY
(Donald Slagel) **SMC 18**
An olio of songs from England, Hungary, Ireland, Jamaica, Middle East, Newfoundland, Nova Scotia, USA. For voices, recorders and classroom percussion.

SKETCHES IN STYLE
(Carol Richards and Neil Aubrey) **SMC 19**
Arrangements for classroom music. For voices, recorders and classroom percussion.

DE COLORES
(Virginia Nylander Ebinger) **SMC 20**
Folklore from the Hispanic tradition for voices, recorders and classroom percussion.

SOMETHING TOLD THE WILD GEESE
(Craig Earley) **SMC 21**
A collection of folksongs for unison treble voices, barred and small percussion instruments, and recorders (soprano and alto).

TEN FOLK CAROLS FOR CHRISTMAS FROM THE UNITED STATES
(Jane Frazee) **SMC 22**
Settings of Appalachian and unfamiliar carols, arranged for voices, recorders and Orff instruments.

SIMPLY SUNG
(Mary Goetze) **SMC 23**
Folk songs arranged in three parts for young singers. They include American folk songs, spirituals and Hebrew melodies.

ALL AROUND THE BUTTERCUP
(Ruth Boshkoff) **SMC 24**
These folk song arrangements are organised progressively, each new note being introduced separately.

RECORDERS WITH ORFF ENSEMBLE
(Isabel McNeill Carley)
Three books designed to fill a need for a repertoire (pentatonic and diatonic) for beginning and intermediate recorder players. Most of the pieces are intended to be both played and danced and simple accompaniments are provided.
Book 1 – SMC 25 **Book 2 – SMC 26** **Book 3 – SMC 27**

TALES TO TELL, TALES TO PLAY
(Carol Erion and Linda Monssen) **SMC 28**
Four folk tales (Indian, African, German and American Indian) retold and arranged for music and movement, with accompaniment for recorders and Orff instruments.

HAVE YOU ANY WOOL? THREE BAGS FULL!
(Richard Gill) **SMC 29**
17 traditional rhymes for voices and Orff instruments. Speech exercises, elaborate settings for Orff instruments using nursery rhymes to show how to play with texts.

FOUR PSALM SETTINGS
(Sue Ellen Page) **SMC 30**
For unison and two-part voices and Orff instruments.

FENCE POSTS AND OTHER POEMS
(Ruth Pollock Hamm) **SMC 31**
Texts for melodies, 'Sound Envelopes', movement and composition. New material for creative melody making and improvisation (including jazz).

THE QUANGLE WANGLE'S HAT
(Sara Newberry) **SMC 32**
Edward Lear's delightful poem set for speaker(s), recorders and Orff instruments (with movement and dance improvisation).

RINGAROUND, SINGAROUND
(Ruth Boshkoff) **SMC 33**
Games, rhymes and folksongs for the early elementary grades, arranged in sequential order according to concepts.

TUNES FOR YOUNG TROUBADOURS
(Dianne Ladendecker) **SMC 34**
Ten songs for children's voices, recorders and Orff ensemble.

DANCING SONGS
(Phillip Rhodes) **SMC 35**
A song cycle for voices and Orff instruments. The contemporary harmonies create a dramatic and sophisticated experience for upper elementary/middle school grades.

KUKURIKU
(Miriam Samuelson) **SMC 57**
Traditional Hebrew songs and dances (including Hava Nagila) arranged for voices, recorders and Orff instruments. Instructions (with diagrams) are given for dances.

CIRCUS RONDO
(Donald Slagel) **SMC 73**
A stylized circus presentation using music, movement, speech, and improvisational technique, for various Orff instruments, recorders and voices.

RRRRRO **SMC 79**
(Polyxene Mathéy and Angelika Panagopolous-Slavik)
Poetry, music and dance from Greece with Greek texts adapted for rhythmic reciting by groups accompanied by percussion and other instruments.

WIND SONGS
(Phillip Rhodes) **SMC 197**
Four songs for unison voices, barred and small percussion instruments.

Other titles in preparation
Full catalog available on request